Grit for the Oyster

250 Pearls of Wisdom for Aspiring Writers

Suzanne Woods Fisher
Debora M. Coty
Faith Tibbetts McDonald
Joanna Bloss

Vintage Spirit

All characters in this work are purely fictional and have no existence outside the imagination of the author and have no relation whatsoever to anyone bearing the same name or names. They are not even distantly inspired by any individual known or unknown to the author, and all incidents are pure invention.

ISBN: 978-0-9815592-2-3

PUBLISHED BY VINTAGE SPIRIT, an imprint of Vintage Romance Publishing, www.vrpublishing.com

Praise for GRIT FOR THE OYSTER

"**GRIT FOR THE OYSTER** is a treasure trove of encouraging words for writers, full of reminders about why God led us to this unique profession and advice from other writers. What a great way to start each writing day!" ~Terri Blackstock, best-selling author whose books have sold over 3.5 million copies; author of *Last Night, True Light* and *Night Light*

"To every Christian writer who's ever felt lonely, inadequate and probably delusional (can't think of any that leaves out), this book throws out a cheerful welcome. In its pages, you'll find a helpful and soul strengthening community. Enjoy." ~David Kopp, best-selling co-author of *The Prayer of Jabez*, executive editor, Multnomah Books

"All of us as writers, whether beginners or experienced, sometimes struggle with procrastination, discouragement, perfectionism, and self doubt. We want to write, we love to write, we feel called to write, but there seems to be so many stumbling blocks along the way. **GRIT FOR THE OYSTER** provides encouragement and inspiration as we encounter these inevitable roadblocks. This is definitely a book you want to keep within close reach as you work. It's like having your own personal writer's group and cheering squad right in your own home!" ~Linda Danis, best-selling author of *365 Things Every New Mom Should Know*

"To those who feel called to write for the glory of God, **GRIT FOR THE OYSTER** is like the 'Writer's Bible.'

This wonderful compilation by four talented authors is a wealth of encouragement and support for aspiring and accomplished writers. I plan to keep a copy on my desk for those times when I need inspiration and motivation in my writing journey. *God bless this little book!*" -Ruth Carmichael Ellinger, award-winning author of *The Wild Rose of Lancaster* and *Wild Rose of Promise*

About the Authors

The four writers behind *Grit for the Oyster* have walked its path.

Suzanne Woods Fisher's work has appeared in many magazines; she is a former contributing editor to "Christian Parenting Today" magazine, author of three historical novels, *Copper Star, Copper Fire,* and *For the Love of Dogs,* as well as a non-fiction book, *Amish Peace in an English Life.* Suzanne and her family live in the San Francisco Bay Area. Find her on-line at www.suzannewoodsfisher.com.

Debora M. Coty is an events speaker, newspaper columnist, internationally published freelance writer of more than eighty articles, Christian humorist, writing instructor, and author of *The Distant Shore, Billowing Sails, Everyday Hope,* and *Mom Needs Chocolate: Hugs, Humor and Hope for Surviving Motherhood.* Also a contributor to *Heavenly Humor for the Woman's Soul* and numerous devotionals, Deb lives and laughs with her husband near Tampa, Florida. She'd love to visit with you at www.deboracoty.com.

Faith Tibbetts McDonald, a former contributing editor to "Christian Parenting Today" magazine, a newspaper columnist, freelance writer, professional speaker, and lecturer at Pennsylvania State University, received the Reader's Pick award for an article published in "Today's Christian Woman" magazine. Faith lives with her husband and three children in Pennsylvania. Visit Faith on Facebook.

Joanna Bloss is the author of *God's Gift for the Grad* (Barbour, 2009) and has written for a variety of publications including "Today's Christian Woman" and "Discipleship Journal." She is a certified personal trainer, graphic artist, and is currently working towards her master's degree in clinical psychology. She lives in the Midwest with her four children. Keep up with her busy life at http://joannabloss.blogspot.com.

Dedication

To aspiring writers
like us...
Perspiring
today
to become
inspiring
tomorrow.

In the crafting
of your exquisite
literary pearl,
may this book be
Grit for *your* Oyster.

"Do not despise these small beginnings, for the Lord rejoices to see the work begin" (Zechariah 4:10).

Table of Contents

FOREWORD by Sally Stuart
Author of *Christian Writers' Market Guide*
www.stuartmarket.com

Over my forty years of working with writers and would-be writers, there are certain things that have never changed. They all need inspiration to get started or to keep writing, and they love to hear the stories of what prompted other writers to start a writing career, to deal with problems or rejections, and to basically just survive the writing life.

Here, at last, is a book that meets and fulfills all those desires in one, easy-to-read volume. Its authors are writers who have worked in the trenches and understand what it's like to face the ups and downs of freelance writing. Better yet, they are willing and able to be open and honest about those day-to-day struggles we can all identify with.

In turn, they will take you to God's Word, apply it to one of the everyday struggles of the writer, bring you back to God in prayer, give you some reflections to help you dig even deeper, and inspire you with the words of other writers who have traveled this same road.

Nothing brings more depth and clarity to our writing than being forced to look inward at those life experiences that have made us who we are. If God has given us a message to deliver in our writing—those things must be worked through our everyday experiences—good and bad. Ultimately they challenge us to become the best writer we can be.

Grit for the Oyster will be a constant reminder that God is perfecting both us and our message by making something beautiful out of each challenge. Then that something beautiful can help transform the lives of our readers. Isn't that what it's all about?

Section 1: Getting Started. Can I? Should I?

"A number of years ago, I came upon 1 Chronicles 28:20. I was struggling with a deadline at the time, and these words spoke to me in a personal way. I have kept the verse, in a personalized form, on my desktop ever since.

'Be strong and courageous, Robin, and do the work. Don't be afraid or discouraged by the number of words you need to write, for the Lord God, my God, is with you. He will not fail you or forsake you. He will see to it that all the work related to this novel is finished correctly' (1 Chronicles 28:20, Robin's Revised Version, adapted from NLT)." -Robin Lee Hatcher, author of *The Forgiving Hour,* www.robinleehatcher.com

"A good writer must be a reader first. Every book I've ever written is the product of a lot of study, prayer, and reflection, most often generated by reading classical and contemporary writers." ~Gary Thomas, author of *Sacred Marriage*, www.garythomas.com

Qualified or Not, Here I Come
Debora M. Coty

"But Moses pleaded with the Lord, 'O Lord, I'm just not a good speaker. I never have been, and I'm not now, even after you have spoken to me, I'm clumsy with words'" (Exodus 4:10, NLT).

After 430 long years of captivity, God chose Moses, a fumble-tongued, murderer turned nomad, to speak on His behalf and lead the Israelites from their bondage—to become their long prayed-for emancipator. What was Moses' reaction? "Who am I to go?" (Exodus 3:11, CEV). In other words, "What on earth are you thinking, Lord? You should find somebody else; I'm the wrong person for this job!"

There it is—the Moses Mantra: I'm not qualified for this job, Lord!

The Bible is full of people who, by outward appearances, weren't qualified for the work to which God called them. Saul, a donkey herder, was chosen by God to be the first king of Israel. David, a musical shepherd, was called to be the next warrior king.

Rahab, the Gentile prostitute, was hand-picked by God to become an important link in the ancestral (Jewish) lineage of Jesus. Mary was a carefree teenager when she was chosen as the nurturer of God's own son.

Paul, a dreaded vigilante against Christians, was appointed to become the greatest evangelist of all time. A mere fisherman, Peter, was called to become the foundation of the worldwide Christian church.

Could it be that we of *other* professions could possibly be called by God to further His kingdom via the written word?

Shortly after my first three magazine articles came out, a conversation with an acquaintance at church stopped me cold.

"Did I overhear you say you've been published?" the wannabe writer asked, drawing her tall frame close to peer down at my short, stubby self.

"Why, yes," I naively replied, smiling in anticipation of the accolade sure to follow.

"And what exactly qualifies *you* to be a writer?" (She knew I was an occupational therapist and piano teacher.) "Did you major in journalism in college?"

"Well, no..."

"Were you an English major?" she asked in an impeccably crisp tone. "Or Literature, perhaps?"

"Not exactly." Had someone suddenly cranked up the furnace?

"Then how, may I ask, are you qualified to be a writer?" She stood glaring, arms crossed and lips pursed.

For once in my life I was speechless. Struck by a bolt of divine inspiration, I shook my head. "I guess I'm not. You're absolutely right. I'm *not* qualified to be a writer. But let me tell you something really funny—there are three editors who *think* I am!"

When I first felt God's still, small voice nudging me toward writing, I heralded the Moses Mantra loud and clear. Me, write? I've been working in other jobs for twenty-five years; I'm too old to learn something new. You've got the wrong gal, Lord. It's been w-a-y too long since English class—I wouldn't know an ellipsis from an eclipse. My participles would dangle like fishhooks, and my metaphors would be messier than my son's bedroom.

But that little voice inside wouldn't be quieted.

You know the rest. It's your story, too. That little voice inside you wouldn't go away either, and so here you are, pursuing your writing dream. Just like Moses, your excuses melted away, and your mantra instead became: Whatever you will, Lord, that I will do.

And with every slash of the pen and tap of the keyboard, God reminds us, "My grace is sufficient for you, for My power is made perfect in weakness" (2 Corinthians 12:9, NIV).

Prayer: *Still, Small Whisperer to my Soul, fill me with Your power and Your peace and guide my written words to always glorify You. Amen.*

Reflection

During the past year, when have you uttered the "Moses Mantra?" (Also known as: I'm not qualified for this job, Lord!)

What aspect of writing is God's still, small voice nudging you to pursue—devotions, short stories, magazine articles, books, poetry?

List three specific steps you can take to become more qualified in this area.

"Every time you write, you add more to your abilities as a writer. Don't worry so much about being a beginner. As a matter of fact, statistics show that 99.97% of writers start out as beginners. No need for you to ever have to justify or apologize for being a beginner. The beginning? It's actually a very exciting place to be. It's a place full of promise, anticipation, hope—everything thrilling!" ~Rhonda Rhea, speaker, radio personality, humor columnist, author of *High Heels in High Places,* www.rhondarhea.org

"Stay determined, even after you get published. Preston Sturges, the legendary writer-director, once said, 'When the last dime is gone, I'll sit on the curb with a pencil and a ten-cent notebook and start the whole thing all over again.' Try to keep that attitude, no matter where your writing goes." ~ James Scott Bell, best-selling novelist, former fiction columnist for *Writer's Digest,* and author of *Write Great Fiction: Plot & Structure,* www.jamesscottbell.com

"If you're a new writer, just starting out on this incredible journey, face the fact that it easily can be a one-step forward, two-steps backward adventure. Fortify yourself with plenty of prayer, patience, and perseverance—unless you're the exception, you'll eventually need a lion's share of each. Be prepared to deal with the bitter as well as the sweet. But don't let the frustrations and disappointments ever overshadow your joy in and your appreciation for the gift you've been given. And don't forget that it is a gift. Nothing more, nothing less." ~BJ Hoff, best-selling author of *Mt. Laurel Novels,* the *Mountain Song Legacy Series, An Emerald Ballad Series,* and the *American Anthem Series,* www.bjhoff.com

"I used to compartmentalize my writing from my Christian life. I wrote secular romances with sex and profanity, and because I was publishing everything I wrote, I told myself God was blessing it. But He wasn't. God never blesses sin, and my writing was not only sinful, I believe it led others into sin. After 32 books published, the Lord orchestrated things in my life to draw me back to Him. I finally realized that He wants every area of our lives. He had given me the gift of writing so that I could glorify Him, but I was using that gift to do just the opposite. I got down on my knees and repented and told the Lord I didn't want to write anything else that didn't glorify Him. Since that time, He has blessed my work immensely. I wish I'd committed my writing to Him years earlier." ~Terri Blackstock, bestselling author of numerous books including *Night Light*, www.terriblackstock.com

"God will provide the words like manna in the wilderness. God didn't dump a year's worth of food on the Israelites. He provided enough for *that day*. That's how He provides His words to me...enough for that day." ~Tricia Goyer, author of *Life Interrupted: The Scoop on Being a Young Mom*, www.triciagoyer.com

Paying Attention

Suzanne Woods Fisher

"When I consider your heavens, the work of your fingers, the moon and the stars which you have set in place, what is man that you are mindful of him, the son of man that you care for him?" (Psalm 8:3-4, NIV).

Jesus grew up in a dusty, tiny, "can-anything-good-come-out-of-Nazareth?" type of town. He never traveled more than a few hundred miles from Nazareth, and while He was exposed to Roman occupation of Israel, most of the people in His world shared His religion, His language, His customs.

Out of that narrow, provincial upbringing, (almost laughable when we consider His impact on the world), Jesus was able to touch the hearts of thousands during His brief ministry, connecting to people in a profound way.

How? Jesus paid close attention. Nothing escaped Him. A timid woman who reached out to touch the hem of His garment because she believed it would heal her, the lilies in riotous bloom in the springtime, a withered fig tree alongside of the road, a short man who climbed a tree to catch sight of Him. (Luke 8:42-48, Matthew 6:28, Mark 11: 12-14, 20-26, Luke 19:1-6).

Jesus noticed the motives behind people's actions, the doubts that plagued their hearts, the unspoken questions they had for God. Jesus took the world that He knew on earth, the world that His audience was familiar with, and drew parallels from ordinary experiences with the heavenly kingdom.

Very ordinary experiences. His examples were simple, largely consisting of evidence of a material world, while pointing people to a new reality—the Kingdom of God.

We, too, have a world around us that is waiting to be noticed. Look for inspiration in the places in which God puts you. Ordinary places. Ordinary people.

Develop eyes and ears to see and hear life on a deeper level. Once you begin, you'll be amazed at the sources of inspiration you'll encounter. I can guarantee that life will never seem quite the same. Instead, it will be filled with meaning. Just as God *intended* it to be.

Author Anne Lamott carries an index card and pen in her back pocket every time she leaves her house. Expectantly. Attuned for just the right word, or remark, or circumstance that can be grist for her mill.

She's training herself to pay attention.

Prayer: *Lord God, all day today, help me to look beyond responsibilities and routines, the tangles of daily worries. May I get past my own stingy limitations and remember to open my eyes and pay attention. Thank You in Jesus' Name. Amen.*

Reflection

What is one thing you can do to teach yourself to pay

closer attention to the world around you?

How does it inspire you to know that Jesus had such remarkable insights even though He never traveled much? How does that knowledge affirm you?

"All we can—or should—do is to write the book of our heart, the story for which God gives us a passion. That is our best hope of catching a wave." ~Deborah Raney, author of *A Vow to Cherish*, www.deborahraney.com

"I remember when I first started my freelance career. The hardest part was getting started. I always allowed distractions to keep me from writing. Then one day I decided it was time to make an appointment for my writing, just as I did with doctor appointments. In less than 30 days I had formed a new habit and my writing time was no longer an issue." ~Alyice Edrich, author, editor, *The Dabbling Mum®* website, www.thedabblingmum.com

"Always ask for God's help when you're writing. Stop if you need to and pray or read the Bible until you receive an answer. Then praise Him and give Him glory." ~Audrey Hebbert, author of *Green Light Red Light*, www.audreyhebbert.com

"Prayer was important to me as I began a career in writing and is certainly a pillar for me today. As I continually lift my heart's desire to the Father and seek His direction, He faithfully leads me and gives me great peace in the process." ~Karol Ladd, best-selling author of *The Power of a Positive Woman*, www.positivemom.com

"Whatever you do, don't get discouraged! Sometimes you have to knock and knock and knock before the right door opens. Patience is everything in getting published..."
~Liz Curtis Higgs, author of 26 books, including her best-selling *Bad Girls of the Bible* series, www.lizcurtishiggs.com

The Big Picture
Faith Tibbetts McDonald

"What does man gain from all his labor at which he toils under the sun?

...The teacher searched to find just the right words, and what he wrote was upright and true: Of making of books there is no end...but here is the conclusion of the matter: Fear God and keep his commandments, for this is the whole duty of man."

(Ecclesiastes 1: 3; 12:10–14, NIV).

Months after Hurricane Katrina hit, I worked with a clean-up crew in New Orleans to help gut a house that had soaked in eight feet of water for five weeks in post-Katrina flooding. I carted a wheelbarrow load of moldy insulation and crumbled plaster to the growing mound of trash by the curb in front of the house. As I dumped the debris, I noticed that the only whole, recognizable item in the pile was a book which was propped to reveal the title: *The Big Picture.*

Juxtaposed with the pile of trash, the title acted as a piercing and ironical caption. It prompted me to think about life: Everything we own or touch will eventually be trashed. Is *that* the big picture?

For me, a writer, questions about writing dreams are inextricably linked to questions about life. I began to think about the big picture for articles I've written and books I hope to write. Every page I've ever written, or ever hope to write, will, in one way or another, end up in a trash heap. Is *that* the end of my labor?

These thoughts did not feel as good as the rush I'd felt a few months earlier when I'd visited an acquaintance's home and noticed one of my articles—poignant sentences highlighted—posted prominently on her fridge.

At the debris pile, as I leaned on the upended wheelbarrow's handles, I realized that it's easy to picture the final product of writing labor. I imagine the idea sorting, the computer keys' staccato clicking, and the rummaging through the thesaurus as culminating in polished, printed pieces. I can visualize manuscripts repeatedly sent to and sometimes rejected by editors as evolving into a printed book, prominently displayed in a local bookstore. And, of course, I can imagine an adoring, autograph-seeking crowd as they stand in line to purchase it.

But even *if* that happens (I like to dream big), that scenario isn't really the end of the story. As I looked at that book on the trash heap, I realized that all the copies of any book I might write will eventually be discarded. Is that the result of my toil? The big picture that God wants me to see?

Should I write with that end in mind, hoping that on their journey to the heap, my words might be highlighted, posted on a fridge, treasured in a heart? What *is* the big picture for me? With the trash heap in mind, how do I find and fit into a picture that is compelling enough to keep me engaged in this activity of placing black marks on white paper?

I'm not the first author to ask these questions. The writer of Ecclesiastes asked questions like these centuries ago. After thinking them through, he assigned value to a writer's pursuit to write wise, upright, true words that prompt heart-change. However, he realized that of even higher priority is the pursuit of fearing God and keeping His commandments.

Often, rapt in doggedly pursuing writing goals, I begin to see writing successes as the big picture. However, while concentrating diligently on the aspects of my work that I can measure in time, I must remember that the pursuit that will stand the test of time is the pursuit of loving God. *That* is the big picture.

Worship first. Then write.

Prayer: *Lord, help me write as an expression of worship. Don't let the vigor with which I pursue writing goals be greater than the vigor with which I pursue You. May the ideas I express in writing be true. Purify the motives that drive me. May the attitudes that govern my thoughts please You. Amen.*

Reflection

What aspects of your work do you think please God most?

What aspects of your work do you need to turn over to God so He can purify them?

Name one thing you can do *today* to ensure your work matters beyond time.

"You must want to enough. Enough to take all the rejections, enough to pay the price of disappointment and discouragement while you are learning. Like any other artist you must learn your craft—then you can add all the genius you like." ~Phyllis A. Whitney, mystery writer, recipient of the Grand Master Award, www.phyllisawhitney.com

Who, Me? Mistakes?

"What mistakes have I made while seeking publication? Wow, plenty of them. Not understanding the business well enough early on. Not knowing how important writers' conferences are for networking. Not following up on promising leads or relationships (or giving up too early). I can't stress enough how important it is to treat this like a business; a writer has a product to sell, and he or she has to act professionally to get the best deal." ~Nate Kenyon, author of *Bloodstone*, www.natekenyon.com

"A quote that has meant a lot to me was originally on a little plaque in my dad's basement workshop. Later, we had it at our navigational station on our sailboat as we sailed throughout the South Pacific. Now it has a prominent place in my office:

'*Nothing will ever be attempted if all possible objections must be first overcome*' (Dr. Samuel Johnson, an eighteenth century British lexicographer and author)." ~Mary Trimble, author of *Rosemount* and *McClellan's Bluff*, www.whidbey.com/marytrimble

Excerpt from "Push Through the Pain of Publishing"

"I liken the writing process to giving birth. Something very precious is conceived in your imagination, and it begins stirring in your soul. It grows so heavy in your spirit that there's absolutely no ignoring it. The only option you have is to feed it, nurture it, and deliver it, pushing through the labor pains until your book is brought to life." ~Shannon Etheridge, best-selling author of *Every Woman's Battle* and the *Loving Jesus Without Limits* series, www.shannonetheridge.com

"If you are dyslexic and have ADHD like me, you can still write books. Turn off the computer screen so you can't see your mistakes and write! Don't edit; don't correct spelling or punctuation. Keep writing so you don't lose a single thought! Correct it later. Write what you are passionate about. Don't try to think up some new thing. Write everything you think on the subject no matter how ridiculous. Tell stories. Paint word pictures. Make things up. Quote other people. Now turn on the screen and start editing it all to make sense!" ~Sue Buchanan, humorist. author of *The Bigger the Hair the Closer to God,* www.suebue.com

No More Detours

Joanna Bloss

"I press on toward the goal to win the prize for which God has called me heavenward in Christ Jesus" (Philippians 3:13-14, NLT).

I can't point to a specific date and time that God called me to be a writer. But for fifteen years, I've just *known* that writing is one of the things He wants me to do. I would love to say that from the moment I knew this I've done so diligently and that both the volume and income of my writing has risen steadily as the years have passed.

However, if I were to graph my progress, it would look more like a jagged mountain range (think Grand Tetons) than a slowly ascending slope. The truth is, I've taken a few detours from time to time. Okay, I've taken a lot of detours a lot of times.

Why? One reason is that I have what experts refer to as a "deficit." A deficit of attention. You might laugh and say, "I do, too," but honestly, I have battled ADD my entire life. And while there are some definite upsides to this "ailment" (like creativity, bursts of energy, and lack of boredom), it can be extremely frustrating to feel completely overwhelmed by the sheer volume of unfinished tasks that constantly surround me.

We live in a world that values being task-oriented and highly productive. I am neither. Writers do not get paid for being neither, nor do they find it highly satisfactory to begin tasks and not finish them.

That's the bad news. But the good news is that for me this is changing. Over the years I've learned some strategies for managing the attention deficit and increasing my writing productivity.

1.   *Contentment with the way I'm wired.* I don't necessarily start and finish tasks in the way that others do them, but I am capable of both. I've found the methods that work for my type-A writing buddies (who write several thousand words every day) do not work for me. For example, I generally start three or four pieces at once, work on them a little bit at a time, then finish them as the deadlines arise. This would drive my friends crazy, but it works for me.

2.   *The importance of setting long-term goals.* I set goals like "get published in a certain magazine" or "write xx number of articles in a given time" or "get a fiction novel published before I die." Okay, so these aren't exactly Pulitzer prize-winning ideals, but I have prayerfully considered the goals God wants me to achieve, and I've set my sights accordingly.

3.   *The necessity of getting focused short-term.* No team would take the field without first meeting with the coach, and no actor would take the stage without getting into character. It might not surprise you to know that I

do not, as many writers suggest, set a goal of writing a certain number of words per day. I've found the following strategy to be very helpful for my writing productivity: I begin each (okay, most) of my days with a "team meeting." God and I are the only ones present, but I spend this time focusing first on Him, then His word, and finally on the specific tasks He wants me to accomplish that day. This has dramatically transformed my level of productivity.

4.   *The value of connecting with others.* Connecting with other writers is the second most important thing I've done to maintain productivity. I ask them to hold me accountable, help me maintain deadlines, and keep me on task. Connecting in some way—every day—to the writing life, whether it be through reading writers' blogs, books on writing, or reading up on the industry, also keeps me focused, inspired, and productive.

5.   *"Little things" really do matter.* I typically have the attention span of a five-year-old. Noises, sounds, bright lights, and strong smells can be both distracting and irritating to me. I've discovered that creating the right environment greatly enhances my ability to write. This means that when I need to concentrate, I silence the incoming mail chime on my computer, or better yet, get offline altogether. I attend to dripping faucets and needy children ahead of time, and I try not to answer the phone or doorbell when I'm in process, because next thing I know I'll be simultaneously sorting through mail and placing a catalog order while I chat with my sister. Sometimes the best thing is to just leave the house, so I have my favorite writing spots that allow me to hunker down and get some real work done. (Somehow the bustling activity of a coffee shop isn't nearly as distracting to me as the seven loads of laundry screaming for my attention.)

Sometimes I look back over my fifteen-year career and feel discouraged that I haven't accomplished more. When this happens I've found that Paul's wise words in Philippians apply to my writing life as well: "Forgetting what is behind and straining toward what is ahead I press on toward the goal to win the prize for which God has called me heavenward in Christ Jesus" (Philippians 3:13,14).

Whether or not it's ADD, I suspect that most writers struggle with *something* that impedes their progress. Whatever yours is, remember to embrace the way God uniquely wired you and depend on Him to help you reach your goals.

Press on.

Prayer: *Dear Father, even though it doesn't always make sense to me, I thank You for the way You wired me, and I know You did so intentionally. Help me to embrace my strengths, accept my weaknesses, and trust You to lead me to accomplish each and every goal You've set before me. Amen.*

Reflection

In what way has God uniquely wired you to write?

What distracts you and keeps you from meeting your writing goals?

Which "little things" can you alter to help you become more productive in your writing?

"NOW GET BUSY, GO WRITE AND QUIT MAKING EXCUSES. A badly finished manuscript can be fixed. A blank sheet of paper? Not so much." ~Kristin Billerbeck, author of *A Girl's Best Friend*, www.kristinbillerbeck.con

"Start small but dream big. Set your goals high, but begin by just taking baby steps and see where God leads you." ~Linda Danis, best-selling author of *365 Things Every New Mom Should Know*

"Too many of us wait to do the perfect thing, with the result that we do nothing." ~William Feather, publisher

"As the mother of young children, I had difficulty when my little ones interrupted me just because my attention was focused elsewhere. Invariably, it seemed, they'd come up and demand my attention just when a chapter or dialogue was really taking off. A friend told me to keep a wet washcloth nearby. If my children insisted on my attention, I would turn around and lovingly wash their faces. They quickly learned the difference between an emergency and attention-getting behavior." ~Dorothy Solomon, author of *Predators, Prey, and other Kinfolk*, www.dorothyallredsolomon.com

"Write everyday, read everyday. It's that simple." ~A.P. Fuchs, author of *Light at the Edge of Darkness*, www.apfuchs.com

Will Work For Words

Debora M. Coty

"Whatever you do, do your work heartily, as for the Lord, rather than for men" (Colossians 3:23, NAS).

I was a late bloomer. God didn't call me to write until my youngest chick flew the coop when I was in my mid-forties. He sparked the internal flame as I was reading about a writer's contest in a magazine at the dentist's office. I recalled as a teen, third on the list of five things I wanted to accomplish before entering Glory was to write a book.

Unfortunately, life intervened and that goal was back-burnered. By the time my desire was rekindled, my only qualifications were ferocity for reading and desire to follow God's leading, whatever unchartered terrain the path wound through.

When God verified my calling, I was mortified! The jungle of professional writing appeared to be infiltrated with a profusion of man-eaters!

In preparation for this new ministry (providentially inspired writing *is* a ministry), I heartily threw myself into my work. I took crash courses on grammar and punctuation and devoured every "how to" material I could find on the writing industry, various genres, writing styles, and marketing.

Studying my favorite magazines, I red-penned whatever spoke to me in articles I liked. Those magazines became my long-term marketing goals. For the short-term, I knew I had to break into the pony leagues before stepping up to the plate in the majors, so I began submitting to smaller magazines that accepted entire manuscripts. Queries intimidated me, so I gradually worked up to them, warming up my literary swings for the tough pitching.

I approached writer's conferences loaded for bear, equipped with a briefcase full of published clips, articles to market, and book proposals. What I lacked in finesse, I made up for with hard work, common sense, and a *lot* of prayer. I was astounded at the number of people who came empty-handed. What a waste of a tremendous opportunity to market work and learn what editors wanted face-to-face!

Frustrated would-be writers are everywhere. I'm sure you have found, as I have, that when people find out that you write, inevitably they have a cousin or brother, or they themselves are the next Jane Austen just waiting for their big break. And they make it sound so easy—throwing together a few sentences for an article or sitting down and zipping off a fistful of chapters for a book. *Anyone* can write, right?

The reality is, perhaps nearly everyone can write, but not everyone is a *writer*. God equips and calls only special people to become writers. Besides natural talent and potential skill, He looks at intangibles like the heart. Can your love for Him and aspiration to further His kingdom best be utilized through the written word? If so, a burning desire is deeply implanted that becomes almost like an addiction. Add a dash of stubbornness and a hefty wallop of perseverance, and you've got a writer in the making. And if you're reading this, my friend, you are probably one of the chosen.

Yes, it is possible to make a living as a writer, if that's what God has called you to. If you're a freelancer, I'd like to share with you one very important lesson I learned early on: Do *not* be squelched by low pay rates. View nothing as beneath you, and consider each publishing experience as a step up to the next level. Three cents per word may not seem worth your time, but you'll be rewarded with a nice clip to add to your repertoire—bait to help you land a much bigger fish on the next expedition. "Insider" books and trade periodicals like "Writer's Digest" and "Writers' Journal" offer a profusion of tips on tapping into the market and selling more freelance work.

On those dreaded low days when you thrust a crumpled wad of rejection slips into your file and you begin to doubt that God could *ever* use your writing skills to influence anyone toward His kingdom, read the book of Psalms. The poems and songs penned by David *thousands* of years ago still comfort and encourage believers in a mighty way today.

There's power in the written word, and when infused with God's blessing, those words—your words—pierce flesh and bone and touch hearts with the very fingers of God.

Prayer: *Author, Sovereign Creator, and Infuser of the powerful written word, help us to always remember we are working for You, on an eternal scale, rather than being shackled by the limits of this temporary world. Amen.*

Reflection

What steps have you taken to prepare for your writing career?

Identify three writing goals for the upcoming year.

Consider your writing to date and thank God aloud for at least one work that you feel was infused with His blessing.

"Just show up at your desk, day after day after day—the more likely you are to start having more ups than downs." ~Deborah Raney, author of *Remember to Forget*, www.deborahraney.com

"Exalt the Lord in ALL things—the words you write, the things you say, the acts you do. God forbid that we write holy words and lead unholy lives." ~Donna Shepherd, author of *Topsy Turvy Land*, www.donnashepherd.com

Excerpt from "The Trouble with Success"

"A dozen years ago my first book landed on a bestseller list. My elementary school teachers prepared me for numerous things, but not for success. If asked who would become a successful writer, they would have singled out girls with horn-rimmed spectacles who sat upright in their chairs, finishing assignments on time. My report cards prepared me for failure." ~ Phil Callaway, humorist, author of *Laughing Matters* and *Family Squeeze*, www.philcallaway.com

"The psalmist and the prophet never studied creative writing, never attended writers conferences, or poured over the myriad of publishing guides available to the aspiring writer, yet some of the most beautiful and profound writing ever penned was written under the influence and prompting of God Himself." ~Ruth Carmichael Ellinger, award-winning author of *The Wild Rose of Lancaster* and *Wild Rose of Promise,* www.ruthellinger.com

"I've learned that what's easy to read is hard to write, and what's easy to write is hard to read. I'm a steward of words, and I'm accountable to God for how I arrange them. That's the best reason for working hard at rewriting: 'Work at it with all your heart, as working for the Lord, not for men (Colossians 3:23)." ~Randy Alcorn, founder of Eternal Perspective Ministries, author of *Heaven*, www.epm.org

Missing the Point
Suzanne Woods Fisher

"His master replied, 'Well done, good and faithful servant! You have been faithful with a few things; I will put you in charge of many things. Come and share your master's happiness!'" (Matthew 25:21, NIV).

In a familiar parable told by Jesus, a wealthy master gave his three servants different portions of talents to care for while the master was away on an extended business trip. The Greek word for talent ("talanton") actually referred to a monetary unit or a weight. In Jesus' day, one talent of silver or gold would have equaled a vast amount of money, nearly unattainable.

In this parable, Jesus was driving home the point that each servant was meant to make the most out of the master's investment. They should anticipate a day when they would need to account for their bestowed responsibilities. The servant who was given five talents (servant #1) doubled his portion and received his master's approval and blessing. So did the one allotted two talents (Servant #2). In fact, the master's response to each of these servants was identical. He was delighted!

But then came servant #3. This fellow has only been given one talent to invest. Knowing the master as well as he thought he did, he feared the master's response. Instead, he buried the talent but ended up losing his master's favor.

There is another angle to this parable, one that is particularly suited to those of us with a fondness for philology. The modern use of the word "talent"—a natural ability or endowment—dates back to this very parable. The scripture passage of Matthew 28:14-30 is even referenced in Webster's Dictionary under the word "talent."

Slide the modernization of "talent" into the parable. Substitute your writing capacity as the portion of talent God has given to you. How much has he given to you? Five portions? Two? One?

My first response is to wonder why I have been given a rather small portion of talent. "Lord, why wouldn't you have granted me five portions? Why a measly two portions? Or one?" I whine silently. That little seed of discontent with my skimpy portion is always lurking around, ready to sprout.

In *Grace (Eventually)*, author Anne Lamott describes her battle with writer's jealousy: "I know that when someone gets a big slice of pie, it doesn't mean there's less for me. In fact, I know that there isn't even a pie, that there's plenty to go around, enough food and love and air. But I don't believe it for a second. I secretly believe there's a pie. I will go to my grave brandishing a fork."

With her candid cheekiness, Anne Lamott has missed Jesus' point.

My college friend, Ginny, can write circles around me. Prose flows from her effortlessly. She once wrote a book review that was more interesting to read than the actual book! I think of Ginny when I consider this parable. She, with her five talents, me, with my...less than five.

And I have entirely missed Jesus' point.

The master never asked the servants if they were satisfied with their allotments. Scripture says that he gave each according to his ability. The master's only question to the servants was if they made good use of those talents. When Servant #1 and Servant #2 answered affirmatively, the master was thrilled! When the answer from Servant #3 was "no," the master was...so, so not thrilled.

One day, I will stand before the Lord and show him what I've done with my allotment of talent. Oh, I don't want to be like Servant #3 and lose God's blessing and approval. I long to hear those same words of delight he gave to Servant #1 and Servant #2. Don't you?

Prayer: *Giver of Gifts, I commit my writing to You today and every day. Teach me and change me, Lord. Bless my efforts as I continue to improve my craft and make the most of the talent You gave to me. Amen.*

Reflection

What talents, interests, and passions does God want you to put to work today?

Have you given your writing talent wholly and completely to God for His use?

If so, when? What kind of effect did it have on your writing?

Excerpt from *The Downside of Success*

"Most of us have dreams of succeeding in the writing-publishing business. For some, fame satisfies; for others, money brings excitement. Mixed with that is the sense of well-being and doing what we feel God has called us to do. What happens when we begin to achieve that success? The downside awaits us—all of us. Once we begin to publish regularly, especially books, we need to be aware of what follows. The more name recognition we receive and the larger our book sales, the more frequently we encounter the dark side." ~Cecil Murphey, best-selling author, speaker, and conference teacher, http://themanbehindthewords.com

"A writer's tools are his words—add to them daily, memorize their meanings, and learn to spell them like a first place kid in a spelling bee." ~DiAnn Mills, author of *Lightning & Lace*, www.diannmills.com

"I didn't think I had much writing talent, but I gave God my few loaves and fishes. As I prayed and wrote, I watched God multiply my writing to feed thousands of readers. Offer God what you have. That's all He wants. Then watch Him bless others through your words." ~Lydia E. Harris, freelance writer, national columnist of "A Cup of Tea with Lydia", www.lydiaeharris.com

"I've discovered that this writing game is fun! It's possible to get published, even if you're a nobody who knows nobody. I did it, and a number of my friends have done it, too. You can, if you're willing to work hard and work smart." ~Randy Ingermanson, publisher, *Advanced Fiction Writing E-zine*, Christy award-winning author of *Transgression* and *Oxygen*, www.ingermanson.com

"Getting published is a lot like losing weight. I'm sorry to say there isn't a twelve step program to success. We all know what to do; it's just having the discipline to stick with it. Dedicate yourself to sitting in the chair and writing your story. Now is not the time for editing. Just get the story down in all its glory. You can polish and spit-shine after you've written those two magical words—THE END." ~Teresa Slack, author of *Evidence of Grace*, www.teresaslack.com

Finding My Writer's Voice
Faith Tibbetts McDonald

"A voice is calling, 'Clear the way for the Lord....'" (Isaiah 40:3, NAS).

One afternoon I was driving across Pennsylvania, and I stopped at a rest stop to stretch my legs. In the rest stop foyer, surrounded by the vague buzz of conversation, I was startled to hear a voice I recognized. Ten years had passed since I'd heard that voice. Yet instantly, I knew who was speaking. "Mrs. Howrelook?" I called and scanned the crowd to find my college roommate's mother.

I can talk about pitch. I can mention volume. I can imitate accent. But I can't fully describe the audible intricacies that caught my attention and led to an instant, positive identification of a voice I hadn't heard in a decade. I didn't think: *High-pitched, medium loud, occasional Pittsburgh idiom.* I just knew: It's her!

Like voice in speech, voice in writing is hard to describe, but easy to recognize. It's the quality that draws me to my favorite writers like Anne Lamott, Max Lucado,

Phil Calloway, Frederick Buechner. It's why I read Harper Lee's *To Kill A Mockingbird* again and again. Check out or revisit the book's introduction. The candid, detailed description of Scout's brother draws me in. Not because the narrator's describing something spectacular. It's the sound of her voice that piques my interest.

I love the writer's voice in that story. It reminds me that voice is the unique intangible that makes our writing enjoyable to read and makes our writing ours.

We are born with voice. We develop and hone it by writing, writing, writing (Harper Lee spent three years revising *Mockingbird*) and learning style rules—when to apply them and when to break them. (Writing teachers repeatedly warn students to avoid say-nothing verbs like "got." But look at "got"—front and center in the first line of Harper Lee's Pulitzer prize-winning novel.)

Voice is the gift that will make our writing stand out. A writer's voice can be as recognizable as my college roommate's mother's—for example, think Dr. Seuss.

Our writer's voice, developed and honed, will entice readers, draw readers to God. That's why we call in different genres, publications, and mediums: Clear the way for the Lord.

People have been shouting this message for centuries. Our readers have heard the words before. If we try to spice the message up by slipping in new words, (as I love to do) editors or readers ask: Why use such big words? Can't you talk the way normal people talk?

Why do that, I wonder, when experimenting with locution affords me jubilation?

However, the editors and readers are right. Voice shouldn't call attention to itself. It should call attention to truth. Our task is to tell the truth in our unique voice.

There are only so many true stories under the sun—but they've never been told by me.

When I tell the stories in my voice, I will point to the God who gave me the voice in the first place. And, the gift of God may be that my voice brings readers to a compelling encounter with Him.

I understood the power voice in a new way one day, when in concert, I heard Faith Hill sing the familiar hymn *It is Well with my Soul.* I had heard the song before. I knew the words. I knew the melody. To hear it again could have been a boring round of same old, same old. But Faith Hill's unaccompanied voice, sounding through the auditorium, stunned me. Her voice made that song more than words, more than music. Her voice became the conduit that carried me to touch God. That carried me to the place where I was touched by God.

Let's aspire to the privilege of using our voices to take readers to a place where they can touch God.

Prayer: *Lord, thank you for the writer's voice You've given me. Help me to find it and hone it. Let me use it to tell stories that bring You honor. Amen.*

The Voice of God

Have you ever wondered what the voice of God sounds like? The Bible mentions God's voice over three dozen times. Job 37:5 says that His voice is powerful and Deuteronomy 5:26 says that it commands respect. In John 10:27 Jesus assures us that His sheep know His voice and follow it.

Reflection

What are your favorite writers' voices? What qualities of their voices do you enjoy?

What step can you take to develop your voice to its full potential?

Excerpt from "Don't Let Reviews Get You Down"

"I learned long ago that one of the worst things I could do was read reviews of my books. If they're critical, I beat myself up, sure I can't string a sentence together. On the other side, if the reviews are glowing, I'm far too prone to believe my own press and think I'm the proverbial Cat's Meow. Of course, the reality is someplace between those two absurdities, and the best way for me to keep my feet and heart planted there—in the peaceful reality where I realize God has given me a task and my job is simply to write to the best of my ability—is to not read the reviews. I just keep my focus on the One who called me and on those I'm praying to reach with my stories. Because, when it comes right down to it, that's all that matters." ~Karen Ball, editor, best-selling novelist of *What Lies Within,* www.karenballbooks.com

"I think one of the most important and most difficult things to keep in mind while writing and going through the publishing of a book is to be humble. When the editor tells you something is unclear, chances are it is! The Scriptures tell us to be a joy for our pastors. In a similar way, I think we should be a joy for our editors and publishers. By God's grace, be humble and gracious, thus honoring the Lord in the entire process." ~Martha Peace, Biblical counselor and author of *The Excellent Wife,* www.marthapeace.com

"Write out of the overflow of your own life. Don't write about topics you know little about. Write in the language of the common person. Keep it simple." ~Dr. Gary Chapman, Ph.D., Christian counselor, best-selling author of 20 books including *The Five Love Languages,* www.garychapman.org

"Do it for the One"

"I once had a friend who ran a mission for homeless men. So many of his clients seemed doomed to failure, and there didn't seem to be many success stories that came from his endeavors.

One day, during a conversation, I asked him, 'Out of one hundred men, how many have you actually helped? How many changed their lives?'

He thought seriously for a moment. Then he answered, 'Maybe one.'

I was flabbergasted. 'How do you do this without giving up?'

He smiled and said, 'I do it for the one.'

Writing is a gift. For Christian writers, it becomes something more. It is a ministry. But how can we reach out through our books and touch someone for Him? If we try to stuff our stories with too many spiritual ideas, we can actually dilute the message we want to send.

So, not long ago, after remembering the message I received that day from my friend, I made a change. Now, I 'do it for the one.' In other words, before I start a novel, I ask God to show me the person he wants to reach. Is it someone who didn't have a father growing up and has a hard time trusting Father God? Or is it someone being abused, who needs to know there is a way out? Who is the person God wants to touch through this book? Doing this helps me to keep my focus and makes my message clearer.

For me, 'doing it for the one,' is the way I can use my writing to really 'do it for the One.'" ~Nancy Mehl, author of *In the Dead of Winter,* www.nancymehlbooks.com

"Nothing is wasted in the writer's life. All of our suffering and trials, all of our relationships, all of our deepest, most private thoughts, are fodder for our books. Being a Christian makes that even more true, because Christians see a purpose in everything that happens to them. Writers take that a step further and realize that the lessons they're experiencing can be passed on to their readers. That makes sense out of our suffering." ~Terri Blackstock, best-selling author of *Second Chances* and *Sun Coast Chronicles* series, www.terriblackstock.com

Little Things Become Big Things
Joanna Bloss

"Easy come, easy go, but steady diligence pays off" (Proverbs 13:11, MSG).

One day I answered a local newspaper ad seeking freelancers, confident that it was the perfect job for me. The editor took my inquiry.

"What kind of experience do you have?"

"Uhh..." I stammered, "...none really—but I'm a good writer." She was desperate for freelancers so I was given an assignment. (I didn't realize then just how few writers were willing to work for $20 a story.)

When I decided to hang out my shingle as a writer, it didn't occur to me that inexperience was a problem. After all, I racked up A's in my college writing courses, and I *knew* I was a good writer. That was enough, right?

At least, that's what I used to think. It reminds me of how I felt as a high school student looking for a job. "We'd love to hire you, however...you lack experience." I thought, "Oh yeah? Just how am I supposed to gain experience if no one ever hires me?"

Jesus addresses this issue from a spiritual perspective when He tells the parable of the minas in Luke 19. Essentially He says that as we demonstrate trustworthiness with little things, God will gradually increase our responsibilities, entrusting us with bigger and more important tasks.

Working for the local paper turned out to be a great way to gain experience with, in my case, extremely little responsibility. My articles weren't hard-hitting news stories, and I probably could have made more money *delivering* the papers, but the important thing was the experience I gained. I learned how to do interviews, ask questions, meet deadlines, and a little bit about how a newspaper operates—priceless skills for my writing craft.

Another thing I did in those early days (and still do today) is to offer my services to church ministries. For two years I designed, wrote, edited, and distributed the monthly newsletter for our young mother's ministry. I lost a lot of sleep the night before those newsletters went out, but I gained invaluable experience. I now have in my files two years worth of devotional columns, how-to articles, and interviews that served to hone my writing and editing skills and enrich my clip file.

I also talked shop with other writers. I asked lots of questions and eagerly soaked up their experiences— much easier to do now with a wealth of writing information, writer blogs, and resources widely available over the Internet.

It's been almost ten years since I first hung out that writing shingle. Over the years I've learned a great deal and have been encouraged as God has gradually increased my responsibilities. I've progressed from meager-paying human interest stories to relatively well-paying magazine articles. I've even had my work published in an actual book.

As a writer, if you're feeling more like an inexperienced high school kid than a seasoned professional, have patience. Use your time wisely, be willing to take on small assignments, do them faithfully, then sit back and watch as God rewards the fruit of your labor.

Prayer: *Father, thank you for the writing call You've placed on my life. I pray that You will help me to be patient during this season of inexperience. Help me to prove myself trustworthy with small writing assignments and give me confidence in the promise that You will increase my responsibilities as I am faithful to You. Amen.*

Reflection

What "little things" have you accomplished as a writer?

How might your experience prepare you to take on more responsibility?

What are three things you can do today to gain more experience?

How to Gain Experience:

- volunteer to write a newsletter for your church, school or civic organization
- call your local newspaper and pitch an idea for a human interest story

- start a blog (an online diary) at blogger.com (it's free)
- enter writing contests, such as those at faithwriters.com
- send in material to the "readers contribution" section of your favorite magazine
- write an op-ed piece for the newspaper

Promoting Yourself

"Blogging is an easy, fun, inexpensive way to publish your writing instantly for a worldwide readership. If you write for a specialized market, a topical blog is a *must*; it establishes you as an expert in your field." ~Laura Christianson, publisher of the award-winning *Exploring Adoption* blog, www.laurachristianson.com

"My desire is to build on the body of wisdom God has already given to the church and help broaden that wisdom with a contemporary twist or application. It's arrogant to assume that I know enough, on my own, to view a topic from every angle, without the benefit of other perspectives. Reading helps weed out mere opinions and primes our souls to offer true spiritual direction." ~Gary Thomas, author of *Sacred Marriage*, www.garythomas.com

"I think writers are incredibly brave to send their creations out in hopes of finding a publisher. If you don't take that risk, you are saying 'no' to yourself. You never know until you try. You may never know until you try *again*." ~Vicki Crumpton, Senior Acquisitions Editor, Baker Publishing Group

You're Already Special

Suzanne Woods Fisher

"For he chose us in him before the creation of the world" *(Ephesians 1:4, NIV).*

There's something about being a writer that makes me feel special. It's just not an ordinary career. Not dull. Not average. After all, doesn't "average" sound like oatmeal? Bland, beige, boring. I sort of like feeling special.

Until the Lord gently nudged me one day, causing me to realize I was in danger of seeking after "special-ness" as if it was an idol. Yes, an idol. Maybe not like one of those fat, smiling Buddhas that gather dust on a storeroom shelf, but dangerous all the same because it was the wrong source of fulfillment.

The desire to be special wasn't wrong, but the source was. Isn't that what an idol is? Something we focus on to fulfill our hopes and desires? That desire to be special is a longing deep within, designed to draw me to the heart of God, not to the glare of popping lights.

In a strange paradox, worldly recognition only creates an insatiable appetite. It is the very hunger that this world will never satisfy, not unlike the Turkish Delight candy that Edmund craved in C.S. Lewis' *The Lion, the Witch and the Wardrobe*. It left Edmund hungry for more and more. And more. A craving that could never be satisfied.

God, on the other hand, provides authentic satisfaction to our longings. "You open your hand and satisfy the desires of every living thing," wrote King David (Psalm 145:16, NIV). The need to *seek* special-ness is not biblical. There *is* nothing more we can do to make God care for us, says author Philip Yancey in his bestselling book, *Prayer*. We don't have to seek significance in God's eyes. We already have it. You don't have to *try* to be special. You already are.

Before the galaxies were created, Paul wrote to the church in Ephesus that we were on God's mind. Isn't that astounding? Paul penned those words from a dank Roman prison cell, chained to a Roman guard. There were not many places on earth in which one would have felt less than special. Imagine how raw Paul's wrists were from the tight metal cuffs of the chains, how pasty his skin was from lack of sunlight in the dungeon, how thin and weak he had grown, subsisting on inferior food. Yet Paul did more than merely endure. His faith in a loving God never wavered, not once. Paul never doubted his value, or yours, or mine, in the eyes of God.

If you struggle to rely on this truth, keep on struggling. Pastor Chip Ingraham once told a story about his wife, a woman with very low self-esteem. Throughout their twenty-year marriage, he has seen her work hard to grasp and believe the truth that she is special in God's eyes. Not easy, not over, but she perseveres in that grasp, clinging to the promise of God, because Scripture tells her she is cherished.

Writing *is* special. It is a unique vocation with many fringe benefits. We are allowed a glimpse into many peoples' lives, we weave together words into meaningful communication, and we have the gift of finding material in all kinds of situations in life.

But we need to write for the right reasons, to glorify God.

Prayer: *Author of Words, thank You for giving me a desire to write. Mercifully intervene with Your still, small voice to remind me to keep the desire to write focused on You alone. Amen.*

Reflection

What motivated you to become a writer?

Has that motive met your expectations?

If not, have you considered that you need to change the reason you write?

"Let's say the Bible was taken as our writing handbook. We would learn that lists of do and don't are useful but not in big demand (Leviticus) while lists of your lover's attributes are not useful but always get a buzz (Song of Songs). We would learn that formal and elegiac endures (Isaiah) while personal and embarrassing also endures (proto-blogger David). That cranky (James), wandering (Peter), factual (Luke), quiet (Ruth), wry (Jonah) and weird (Ezekiel) can all deliver in their own way. We would learn that God has used many voices and topics to reach many—and for once, just rest in that. We'd be grateful that one sentence of truth can change a life. For me today it's 'But in your hearts, set apart Christ as Lord.'" ~David Kopp, best-selling author, executive editor, Multnomah Books

"I would rather a writer sound real and authentic than educated or well-spoken. Speaking the truth gets all caught up in fog and fussiness when writers try to sound eloquent and refined." ~Jean E. Syswerda, author of *The Women's Devotional Guide to the Bible*, co-author of the best-selling *Women of the Bible*

"Inspiration. If I waited for inspiration each morning, I would never finish a book. For me, inspiration is similar to a romantic relationship. I am committed to this story, whether I'm in the mood or not, and so I cozy up to it by planting myself in the chair and starting to type. Eventually, creativity flows. It may take an hour, two hours, or two minutes, but that spark usually catches if I let the story know I'm in this for the long haul. It's a spiritual principle of faithfulness that has very practical application." ~Eric Wilson, author of *Flywheel*, www.wilsonwriter.com

Button Writing

"When I first put words on a page, I waited for 'the spirit to move me,' or 'the muse to appear.' One day I asked a seasoned author how her inspiration came.

'I practice button writing.'

All ears, I said, 'And that is...?'

'It's simple. You put your butt on the chair and write.'"

~Sally Jadlow, author of *The Late Sooner*, www.sallyjadlow.com

"If you are willing to work very hard, you just might get published. But if you don't ever see your name in print, it doesn't mean you don't have writing talent. No way! It may mean your proposal and their publishing needs weren't a good match today. Polish your proposal and try another house tomorrow!" ~ Liz Curtis Higgs, author of 26 books, including her best-selling *Bad Girls of the Bible* series, www.lizcurtishiggs.com

A New Name

Faith Tibbetts McDonald

"Jesus looked at him and said, 'You are Simon son of John. You will be called Cephas' (which when translated is Peter)" (John 1: 42, NIV).

Recently, I listened to a book on CD that featured a computer named Translator. The story was so-so; still the idea of a named computer intrigued me. Especially because Translator played a key role in swaying circumstances so that the characters enjoyed a positive outcome.

After hearing about Translator's influence, I fancied that an appropriately named computer might facilitate my writing career so I named my computer Creative Genius. CG for short. As in, "I'm going to my office to spend time with CG." CG and I spend a lot of time together; even so, I'm not sure that my manuscripts have improved dramatically since CG's christening.

Maybe, in real life, it's the writer, not the tool, who benefits from an inspiring name.

Jesus understood the significance of names—for people, that is. When he met a young fisherman named Simon, he immediately dubbed him Peter. Peter means rock. Jesus had selected the impetuous Simon to jump-start the church (Matthew 16:18). With this in mind, Jesus assigned the fisherman a new name which indicated His hopes, dreams, and plans for Peter's place in God's kingdom. Jesus hoped Peter would grow into his name and his calling—become the church leader that Jesus knew he could be.

Even with his new name, Peter floundered. He tried to build the church in the wrong way, in the wrong place, at the wrong time (Luke 9:32, 33). When Jesus needed him to pray, Peter fell asleep (Mark 14:15). Later, Peter hotly denied ever knowing Jesus (Luke 22:57).

Reeling from disappointment in Peter's shortcomings, Jesus might have concluded that the name change hadn't really worked the wonders He was hoping for.

But He didn't. He kept pointing Peter towards the goal. "Blessed are you, Simon son of John...I tell you that you are Peter, and on this rock I will build my church, and the gates of Hades will not overcome it. I will give you the keys of the kingdom of heaven; whatever you bind on earth will be bound in heaven, and whatever you loose on earth will be loosed in heaven" (Matthew 16:17-19).

The name change stuck, and eventually Peter grew into his name.

If Jesus changed your name into a name that indicated His hopes and dreams for your writing, what name do you think He'd select? What do you *wish* He'd select? Writer? Best-selling author? Poet Laureate? (Francine Rivers is already taken. So is Max Lucado.)

I remember the first time someone called me a writer. I blushed. I had enjoyed only modest publishing success. I felt the need to point that out. "I'm not really a writer—I'm an aspiring writer," I said.

The person, someone I respected a great deal, said decisively, "You *are* a writer."

"Maybe I'm a writer," I countered.

"I *know* you are a writer."

The person's confidence that the title "writer" fit propelled me through the difficulties of early writing days.

Later, another person whose opinion I respected immensely described me as a gifted, enjoyable, spirited, and memorable writer.

Now *there's* a writing name worth aspiring to.

The truth is that I don't always turn out manuscripts that make me feel I fit that description. But each time I sit to write, I aspire to that assessment, knowing someday I will grow into my name. Much like Peter grew into his.

When we can't believe in ourselves, we can ask God for courage to live true to His dreams for us. Sometimes, we need someone to help us believe. I've found that if I ask God for encouragement He always provides someone to encourage me, someone to remind me of my writing name.

Prayer: *Dear Lord, when I flounder like Peter, please whisper the writing name You have selected for me. Let me hear You say it. Give me strength and perseverance to aspire to it. Amen.*

Reflection

Do you experience many doubts about your writing ability? What about doubting the call to write?

How would you like your writing to be described? What adjectives do you aspire to?

Has God ever answered your prayer for needed encouragement? In what way? Does that give you hope to pray that prayer again?

"You will be called by a new name that the mouth of the Lord will bestow" (Isaiah 62:2).

"If your goal is to build a name for yourself, every choice you make will be with you in mind. If your goal is to magnify the Lord, you will freely give what's been freely given to you. And it's to this we are called." ~Susie Larson, speaker, author of *Becoming an Uncommon Woman,* www.susielarson.com

Critics Never Change

"Critics are by no means the end of the law. Do not think all is over with you because your articles are rejected. It may be that the editor has his drawer full, or that he does not know enough to appreciate you, or you have not gained a reputation, or he is not in a mood to be pleased. A critic's judgment is like that of any intelligent person. If he has experience, he is capable of judging whether a book will sell. That is all." ~Lavina Goodell, Junior Editor, *Harper's Bazaar,* 1866

"When I'm rejected, I'm in no way dejected. After receiving that dreaded letter declining to use my masterpiece, I look to the future and anticipate a sale to a more fortunate editor." ~Donna Shepherd, author of *Topsy Turvy Land,* www.donnajshepherd.com

"God knows. My heart, my life, my hopes, and His perfect way. God knows!" ~Tricia Goyer, author of *Life Interrupted*, www.triciagoyer.com

Chasing Donkeys

Suzanne Woods Fisher

"The Lord does not look at the things man looks at. Man looks at the outward appearance, but the Lord looks at the heart" (1 Samuel 16:8, NIV).

On an ordinary day, Saul was out on an ordinary task. He was chasing his lost donkeys when he crossed paths with Samuel the Prophet. Saul hoped Samuel, with his direct hotline to God's ear, could lead him to his donkeys, but God had something bigger in mind. Samuel told Saul that he had come to anoint him as the first King over Israel, as the people had requested. Astounded, Saul replied with quivering meekness: "But am I not a Benjamite, from the smallest tribe of Israel, and is not my clan the least of all the clans of the tribe of Benjamin?" (1 Samuel 9:19-21).

The thing was...God didn't *ask* for his credentials. Just his willingness. Notice Saul's focus. It was *entirely* on himself. He never even mentioned God. He wasn't looking to God to equip him for this great task; he was looking at what skills and abilities and pedigree he had to offer. Not much.

A lack of confidence is not the same thing as humility. Undervaluing oneself is just as wrong in God's eyes as exalting oneself. In fact, genuinely humble people have enormous confidence because it rests in a great God.

Too many times, I have allowed a lack of confidence to squelch my desire—even my calling or the sense of being anointed for this work from God—to write. There was a long stretch when I received so many rejections that I lost my enthusiasm. I started to assume that the call to write had just been for a season in my life, and it was time to move on. However, I had no other passion to move on to, and I wasn't getting much of a broadcast from Heaven about what to do next. So I went back to chasing donkeys.

My niece sent me a book called *If You Want to Write* by Brenda Ueland, first published in 1938. Ueland began the first chapter with the remark, "Everybody is talented, original and has something important to say." That one sentence leaped off the page. Isn't *that* how God views each one of us? Suddenly, I felt a loosening inside, and I realized that the only one keeping me from writing was...not an editor, not a publisher...but me. And so I started to write again.

A year later, I received a contract to publish my first novel. Yes, exciting, but it truly didn't compare to the joy I felt in writing the novel. *Just writing.* I finally realized that God wasn't *asking* me to be the best writer in the entire known world, but to *give* Him my best.

If you are called to write then write. Write wholeheartedly. *"For the Lord will be your confidence"* (Proverbs 3:26).

Prayer: *Lord Jesus, help me to go forth and get on with my day's work, knowing that You, alone, are my confidence. Let Your compelling Spirit sweep me up in this incredible lifework You've* *called me to. I am ready for anything through the strength of the One who lives within me. Amen.*

Reflection

What donkeys are you chasing that distract you from work?

Do you have fears about trying to write? What are they?

What are you going to do about those fears?

"As writers in the Kingdom, we're very much like the little boy who gave up his lunch to Jesus. It was all he had, but it was enough. The important thing is, he let it go to the One who could do, oh so much more with it! Jesus did the miracle—but first He asked for the lunch. 'What do you have? Give me that.'" ~Neta Jackson, author of *The Yada Yada Prayer Group*, www.daveneta.com

"In the long run, writing is not about books or deadlines or sales or marketing or success. It's not about getting somewhere; it's about the way you get there. It's about life and how you live it with the people God has given you to love, as you try to be faithful to Him and your gift along the way." ~BJ Hoff, best-selling author of *Mt. Laurel Novels, the Mountain Song Legacy Series, An Emerald Ballad Series*, and *The American Anthem Series*, www.bjhoff.com

"Writing requires discipline; get a plan and stick to it." ~Dr. Gary Chapman, Ph.D., best-selling author of *The Five Love Languages*, www.garychapman.org

"Persistence is vital. It's easy to think a rejection means it's over. In the writing business we must see a rejection as a stepping stone to move on to the next opportunity." ~Karol Ladd, best-selling author of *The Power of a Positive Woman*, www.positivemom.com

Section 2: The Joyful Grind

"No amount of reading, studying, or talking about writing is going to substitute for practice. No one becomes a writer unless they regularly plant their behind in the chair and write. The muse is fickle (and maybe even imaginary). Set a daily goal and stick to it." ~Denise Hunter, author of *Finding Faith,* www.denisehunterbooks.com

"What about taking a few weeks every year (or at least a few days, for crying out loud) just to think a little, to ponder your experiences, to figure out something worth saying?" ~Athol Dickson, author of *River Rising*, www.atholdickson.com

Annual or Perennial?

Joanna Bloss

"But his delight is in the law of the Lord, and on his law he meditates day and night. He is like a tree planted by streams of water, which yields its fruit in season and whose leaf does not wither. Whatever he does prospers" (Psalm 1:2-3, NIV).

My husband and I make an excellent gardening team: he likes to plant things, and I like to see them grow. At least one of us is usually eyeing other gardens for ideas and inspiration. During one particularly beautiful spring, I enjoyed watching a flowering vine climb up my neighbor's mailbox.

"I want one of those," I informed my gardener husband.

He identified the plant—a clematis—and we went to the nursery and picked one out. "It won't look like the neighbor's for a while," he warned me on the way home. "It'll take at least a few years."

Bummer. I was hoping for more immediate gratification. But he was right. It did start out pathetic looking, but four years later my gorgeous purple clematis rivaled anything else growing in our neighborhood.

Any gardener worth his spade knows that annuals are the way to go if you want immediate gratification.

Cheap but colorful. Perennials are more sophisticated. They cost more than annuals, but if you take good care of them, they'll turn up year after year, growing more prolific with each passing season.

I was an "annual" when I first began writing. I started out strong, was able to get quite a few pieces published, and assumed my career was well underway. That was until a couple of rejections showed up in the mailbox, and suddenly my growing season was over. Rejection cooled my heels; my desire waned. My early writing "career" turned out to be very short lived.

One day I was lamenting my lack of productivity when God reminded me of an important gardening principle found in Psalms: trees yield fruit *in season*. The only trees that bear fruit year round are ornamental, and the fruit on them is as tasty as the plastic stuff at the dollar store.

Bearing *real* fruit takes time. There's generally a small window each year for the harvest. I've got some fresh peaches sitting on my counter. These are available fresh off the tree only a few weeks out of the year, but one bite of this delectable treat reminds me that it's well worth the wait.

I've come to accept the fact that I will not always be a productive writer. I've learned to pace myself and to embrace my dormant seasons. Talk to a vineyard owner, and you'll find that what happens to the grapevines during the off-season is equally (if not more) important than what happens to them during the harvest. The external circumstances—ground temperature, soil acidity, precipitation—can all profoundly affect the quality of the fruit.

The same is true for writing. It is highly unlikely that you will always be productive. You *will* get writer's block. You *will* be interrupted. Your children, spouse, family, and/or friends will need you. You will have sick days and will probably face a crisis or two.

Instead of waiting for them to take you by surprise, you might consider intentionally incorporating dormant seasons into the rhythm of your writing life.

A prolific writer friend of mine just completed her thirteenth manuscript. Guess what she did when the manuscript was done, despite facing two deadlines for other projects? She took a month off. Didn't answer e-mail. Didn't take phone calls. She visited her grandkids, puttered in her garden, and took naps. She might have even gone to Disneyland.

My friend has learned one of the secrets of a productive writing career. What you do during the dormant season is as important as what you do during the harvest. Good writing takes time. Great ideas cannot be manufactured.

Do not cave into worldly pressure to produce. Don't get caught up in the frenzy that more is better. "Mass fruit producers" are a dime a dozen. The quality of our fruit is far more important than the quantity.

The psalmist shares two simple secrets for great living and for great writing— plant yourself by streams of Living Water and delight yourself in the law of the Lord.

Do those two things first and whatever else you do will prosper. It's a promise.

Prayer: *Lord, Your Word instructs me to delight in Your Law and to meditate on it day and night. Thank You for the promise that I will bear fruit in season as I draw my nourishment from You. Help me to find a rhythm to my writing life, to put You first, to draw on You for strength, and to be comfortable with down time. Thank You for Your wisdom and grace, without which I would have nothing to write. Amen.*

Reflection

What best describes your writing style: annual or perennial? (An annual starts out strong and lovely, but doesn't last through unfavorable conditions; a perennial is more of a plodder—slow, steady and consistent.)

What personal benefit might you find in slowing your pace and carving out times of rest away from writing?

How can you practically incorporate some intentional down time? (This doesn't mean you stop "working"...just consider the creative edge that might be gained from taking some time away from the keyboard on occasion.)

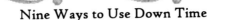

Nine Ways to Use Down Time

- Read a book in the same genre that you write (or one that you'd like to write).
- Try something you've never done before—take a cooking class, go bungee jumping—you never know what idea seeds might be planted.
- Some of my best writing ideas come while I'm cleaning toilets. Do a menial task, and you might find yourself doing some serious brainstorming.
- Go to a bookstore and browse the shelves...what catches your eye? What inspires you?
- Read a classic book by a classic author.
- Copy down ten opening paragraphs to ten different books. Which ones capture your attention? Why?
- Write something (not meant for publication) that is completely out of your comfort zone. If you write fiction, try a how-to article. If you're a novelist, write a poem.

- Complete a task you've neglected too long...organize a closet, have lunch with an old friend, catch up on your scrapbooks, get a haircut, manicure, or massage.
- Take a spiritual retreat...focus on your relationship with God and spend concerted time listening to His voice. ~ Joanna Bloss, http://joannabloss.blogspot.com

"At the outset of my writing career, someone told me, 'If God is in this, don't stop until He says so.' If God is nudging you to write, do it. Work hard to hone your skill. Study the writer's guidelines. Order the sample copies. Attend writers' conferences. Write, write, write. Persevere. If God is in this, don't stop until He says so." ~Grace Fox, author of *Guiding Women to the Truth that Transforms*, www.gracefox.com

"More than any other factor, my goal has been to rightly interpret and present the Bible. I ask myself, 'Is that which I write in keeping with the whole counsel of God?' Seeking to think Biblically resulted in me discovering the idea of unconditional respect toward the spirit of a husband (Ephesians 5:33, 1 Peter 3:2). This truth of unconditional respect had been hidden in plain sight in the Bible for 2000 years. Sadly, culture had removed that notion from the marital radar screen." ~Dr. Emerson Eggerichs, Ph.D., author of *Cracking the Communication Code: The Secret to Speaking your Mate's Language*, www.loveandrespect.com

"Learn to be a good listener. Listeners make the best writers. Listen to your interviewees. Sometime there's another story within the interview that can take your piece to a whole new level." ~Alyce Edrich, author, editor, *The Dabbling Mum*® website, www.thedabblingmum.com

"All five members of my writers' critique group are huge Jane Austen fans. One of our members gave each of us a 6-inch Jane Austen action figure (complete with tiny quill pen in hand). Jane stands sentry near our respective computers, inspiring us with her muse. Whenever any of us experiences a writing or publishing breakthrough, we instantly e-mail each other to share our 'Jane Austen Action Figure Moment.'" ~Laura Christianson, author of *The Adoption Decision* and *The Adoption Network,* www.laurachristianson.com

Kindred Spirits

Debora M. Coty

"For I (Paul) have no one else of kindred spirit who will genuinely be concerned for your welfare" (Philippians 2:20, NAS).

The apostle Paul and Anne of Green Gables were savvy to something many writers are not: We all need kindred spirits. You know, bosom buddies, a Garfunkel to our Simon, a ham to our eggs...a special someone to offer valuable opinions about things important to us.

The confirmation (or correction) we receive from our trusted confidant *improves* us without eliciting that molten lava-bubbling, defensive reaction we've come to know so well when we are ruthlessly critiqued. "You can trust a friend who corrects you" (Proverbs 27:6, CEV).

The difference is that we know the suggestions are being offered in love.

When I first began writing, I felt called to share stories of God's amazing grace notes ("Grace Notes" later became the name of my ministry) in my life although I hadn't a clue how to market them. After asking my Bible Study group to pray with me for guidance, I was approached by a member of the group who knew a local published Christian writer. She offered to ask her friend permission for me to contact her, and thus my first writing buddy relationship was born.

Austine agreed to meet with me periodically at a nearby coffee shop, and over lattes, she graciously mentored me through the early stages of magazine writing nuts and bolts. *No*, you don't have to state copyright—it appears amateurish. *Yes*, you need to go to all the trouble of obtaining each magazine's guidelines and meticulously follow them. *Always* double space, no matter how much paper you think you're wasting. Justify the left margin but *not* the right. *Read* the magazine to which you're submitting. Don't pester editors but *do* contact them after their stated notification times are exceeded.

Because of Austine's "been there, done that" expertise, my evolving articles were professional and polished; I was blessed with ten published pieces that first year. But I felt even more blessed to have a kindred spirit to share tears in disappointment and exalt with me in success.

As my skill level grew, I was able to reciprocate, critiquing her work and offering helpful suggestions. We became true writing buddies (Austine even wrote an article about us called "Why You Need a Writer Buddy: Don't Go It Alone," which appeared in the March/April 2005 issue of *Writers' Journal*). We bounced ideas off each other, mutually detested commas, shared information about contests and periodicals, and best of all, we encouraged one another in a profession which—as you well know—outsiders really don't understand.

Austine eventually had to set aside her writing to focus on pressing domestic issues, and I prayed for God to provide another writing partner. About that time, I attended a writers' conference completely across the country, and because I found no publisher for my new book, I considered it a miserable waste of time and money.

"Why did you send me all the way out here for nothing, Lord?" I railed. But He had a plan. Little did I realize that my roommate at the conference would become my cherished friend and kindred spirit. Suzanne and I *clicked*, and our correspondence has glutted the cyber highway between California and Florida ever since. She cracked open her publisher's door for me to slide in my foot (and my novel), and I edited her new book and synopses. We soon began collaboration on a joint venture.

One very important thing God has taught me about seeking and nurturing kindred spirits—if we approach the relationship thinking only, "What can I get out of it?" or "What can she do for me?"—the match is doomed for failure. One-sided, you-give-and-I'll-take relationships inevitably crash and burn, dishonoring our Heavenly Father in the debris of wounded feelings.

God wants us to emulate His gracious nature: "Do nothing from selfishness or empty conceit, but with humility of mind let each of you regard one another as more important than himself; do not merely look out for your own personal interests, but also for the interests of others" (Philippians 2:3-4, NAS).

Prayer: *Master Creator, thank You for bringing those rare, precious, kindred spirits into our lives. Help us, Father, to look out for the interests of others You place in our paths. Amen.*

Reflection

Who is the kindred spirit in your writing life?

Name two trusted friends from whom you seek and accept correction. Who considers you a trusted friend and believes you have their best interests at heart?

Kindred spirits, like blossoming gardens, require attention and effort to grow and flourish. What are you currently doing to nurture yours?

"Delight yourself in the Lord and He will give you the desires of your heart." (Psalm 37:4 NIV).

Excerpt from "The Trouble with Success"

"When the check arrives, so does a book cover awaiting your approval. You laugh so hard that vital organs begin to hurt because you haven't written a single word of the book yet. Midway through writing the first chapter, a marketing guru calls to tell you how many copies bookstores have already ordered, and your kidneys start to hurt. Expectations aren't so great when they are someone else's." ~Phil Callaway, best-selling author of *Laughing Matters* and *Family Squeeze,* www.philcallaway.com

"I'm just a girl who loves words, who writes to tell stories, earn a bit of money, and glorify my Creator. When I begin to see myself as anything more, my creativity freezes up. I can't write when my words are sandbagged with significance. Humble perspective not only makes me a nicer person, it also frees me to do what I love." ~Rachel Thompson, poet, magazine freelance writer

75

"I've learned I need honest critics and careful editors. But above all I need Christ, who said, 'Apart from me, you can do nothing' (John 15:5). When I work hard at something, I don't want it to amount to nothing. I want it to last forever. I want to hear the Audience of One say, 'Well done.' No payoff could be bigger than that!" ~Randy Alcorn, founder, Eternal Perspective Ministries, author of *Heaven*, www.epm.org

A Writer's Heart

"If you really want to see the Lord use you in a writing ministry, ask him for a writer's heart. Ask for that distinct passion. Even though you may not have the foggiest idea where your writing will end up, or even what kind of writing you will do, you can be passionate about your writing ministry if you start with a clear purpose—His." ~Rhonda Rhea, speaker, radio personality, humor columnist, author of *Purse-uit of Holiness*, www.rhondarhea.com

"Diamonds are nothing more than chunks of coal that stuck to their jobs." *~Malcolm Forbes*

Walk Through the Open Doors
Faith Tibbetts McDonald

"These are the words of him who is holy and true....what he opens no one can shut, and what he shuts no one can open. I have placed before you an open door that no one can shut" (Revelation 3: 7-8, NIV).

My first attempt to write for publication was to submit a piece to "Decision." At the time, I didn't know the odds of being published in that magazine were about one in ten thousand. Good thing. Had I known, I would have assumed the door to that magazine was shut. Tight. I wouldn't have even tried to knock on that door.

However, hopes high, I submitted. The editor promptly dashed my hopes. She liked the article's subject but thought the content was disorganized. (At the time, I didn't know that specific editorial criticism was a scarce commodity that should be treasured.) The editor did not include an invitation to re-submit.

I wondered: *What if I organize the piece and approach "Decision" again?*

So I resubmitted. Eventually, my first published piece appeared in "Decision."

The experience taught me a valuable lesson: Push on doors. Trust God to swing open the writing doors that will allow you to bring Him glory. Trust that the doors that slam shut are shut by Him in your best interest.

Sometimes, the open doors look like they lead to measly opportunities. My publication in "Decision" was followed by an invitation to write about our community in the local weekly. I hesitated. It didn't seem like *much* of an opportunity. But God held that door open and prompted me through. Soon, my community column became a humor column that readers loved—eventually published weekly in five newspapers. I wrote the column for eight years.

Other times, the doors we attempt to go though become as difficult to maneuver as those in an old-fashioned Fun House—an amusement park attraction I remember visiting as a kid. Fun House visitors faced three doors—three ways to enter the indoor playground of wacky rides and mirrors. Usually, I entered through the green door that led to a giant spinning disk. I'd ride the spinning disk, giggling, until the momentum sent me reeling into a padded wall.

Some writing doors lead to the writing life equivalent of spinning disks. Once, an editor telephoned me after reading something I'd written. He *loved* it. Would I please write a similar piece for his magazine ASAP? I promptly pushed aside other projects to stride through that open door. I wrote and submitted the piece. The editor promptly rejected it.

Sometimes, I squeeze through an apparently open door to find I'm staring at the Fun House wavy mirror—a contorted reflection. *Is that me?* I felt like this the time I rewrote a piece three times to please an editor. When it finally appeared in her magazine, flagged with my byline, I didn't recognize it. I searched the dictionary to look up words so I could understand what I'd written.

As writers, we face many doors. We don't know what waits on the other side. Sometimes the door won't open no matter how hard we push. Sometimes, on the other side, we find our efforts rewarded beyond our expectations. Once I submitted a 275-word piece to a magazine. The editor asked me to rewrite it twice. *There are only so many ways you can arrange 275 words*, I thought as I submitted for the third time. That article on teaching kids to be savvy consumers was eventually published, and one day as I listened to the radio, I heard Dr. James Dobson say, "In her article on teaching kids to watch television advertisements, author Faith Tibbetts McDonald says..."

Go through the door that opens today. God will open the doors He wants you to go through and shut the others. You can trust Him.

Prayer: *Father, thank You for opening only the door to publication that will bring You glory. No one can shut it. No one else can get in first. With Your help, I will do my best to walk through every open door I see. Amen.*

Reflection

A salesman acquaintance reminds me that for every sale he expects to make (or to put it in writing lingo, every door you expect to open), he must attempt seven. List seven doors you can knock on this week.

Reflect on your writing career. What doors has God opened for you?

Do you believe God wants you to persevere in knocking on some doors that haven't opened yet? If so, list those doors and ask God for wisdom and strength to continue knocking.

"I remember reading about blocked goals once, and it stuck with me. A blocked goal is a goal that is dependent on other's actions or happenstance. I don't have any control over whether I'll get a contract offered. I can't make people buy my books. I can't make my book sell enough to earn back an advance. I can't control the fickleness of this industry.

What I *can* do is create goals that can't be blocked, like:

1. I will listen to the heartbeat of God and write what He inspires me to write.

2. I will not let writing, by God's strength, overshadow the needs of my family.

3. I will write the best books I can write, always seeking to improve, abounding in humility and teachability.

4. I will be patient when sales wane and trust God's sovereignty.

5. I will promote my books with this motivation: to see the kingdom of God advanced.

6. I will laugh at the unpredictability of this industry and strive to be lighthearted.

7. I will serve others and not let elusive and fleeting fame (if that happens) inflate my head.

8. I will attend conferences, read writing books, and welcome critique.

9. I will serve my readers by praying for them and answering e-mails when God provides time.

10. I will write for the sheer joy of it, not despising unpublished words." ~Mary E. DeMuth, author of *Building the Christian Family You Never Had*, www.relevantprose.com

"If, as a writer, you also hope to sell, KNOW your 'target' audience. Clarify your story's genre and try not to overlap into too many different genres. So much of selling is about marketing, not just about the story. This is often discouraging, but not terrible. Good stories do sell, but good stories that fit marketing requirements sell faster!" ~Gail L.

Fiorini-Jenner, award-winning author, 2005 Willa Chair and Past-President, *Women Writing the West*

"Writing a book is like climbing a mountain. 'The End' looks so far away, but you take it a little at a time. Word by word, step by step, you make your way from The Beginning to The End. And when you get there...the view is great!" ~Ann Parker, award-winning author of the *Silver Rush* historical mystery series, www.annparker.net

"When God opens a door, don't be afraid to walk through." ~Susan Kelly Skitt, author of *The One Year Life Verse Devotional*,
www.livingtheadventurouslife.blogspot.com

"Quiet my heart and clear my mind this morning, Lord, and help me focus on this story that you've given me to write. Keep me from anything that would distract me from the work I need to accomplish, but also let Your Spirit within me discern what is truly a needless distraction and what is important enough that it *should* distract me. Never let me put project above people or worldly gain above things that are eternal." ~Deborah Raney, author of *A Vow to Cherish,* www.deborahraney.com

Making Time for a Cyber Sabbath
Debora M. Coty

"Remember the Sabbath day by keeping it holy. Six days you shall labor and do all your work, but the seventh day is a Sabbath to the Lord your God. On it you shall not do any work..." (Exodus 20:8-10, NIV).

Okay, 'fess up: How many times a day do you check your e-mail?

a. 1   b. 3   c. 6   d. 8 or more

What percentage of an average day do you spend in front of your monitor?

a. 10% or less   b. 25%   c. 50%   d. 75% or more

When was the last 24-hour period you went without turning on your computer?

a. yesterday   b. last month   c. last year   d. never

If you answered (c) or (d) to the questions above, perhaps your computer is dominating more of your life than you realized.

When I worked at McDonalds as a teenager, I got so overdosed with the smells and sight of fast food that when I was off duty, the last thing I wanted was a burger or fries. Somehow, the writing profession doesn't work that way. The more we write, the more we want to write; the more we *need* to write. It's an addiction. The computer absorbs more and more of our attention. We become cyber-junkies.

Part-time writers probably have a harder time fighting the cyber-junkie syndrome than full-timers. Those who have other employment must fit writing time in whenever and wherever they can, whether it's 3 AM or in the middle of Junior's soccer match, whereas full-timers are usually able to establish some sort of schedule. But both struggle with the addiction insipidly taking over their life.

Work evolves into not just five days a week, but gradually six, then seven. The "I'll only be a few more minutes" we tell our kids turns into two hours. They finally give up and find someone else who'll give them attention. Before we know it, they'll be out of the house and will have unequivocally learned the lesson we taught them—that Mom or Dad (or both) would rather spend time with a machine than with them.

Is this the legacy we want to leave behind? Is our primary goal to honor God or to become an honored writer? If we consider our priorities in order of importance—God, family, friends, and work—how can we allow the last on the list to creep up and control the rest?

I realized with a shock that this was the road I was inadvertently traveling when my daughter focused her penetrating brown eyes on the back of my head one day as I was typing and muttered, "I *hate* that computer!"

And then there was the day I lost track of time while editing a manuscript and forgot a much anticipated date with my teenager.

My desire to express myself, to be productive, to meet deadlines, had eclipsed the responsibilities entrusted to me by my Heavenly Father. My precious, limited time on earth was being consumed to the point of neglecting the truly important things—the beloved people—in my life.

That's when I knew something had to change. I needed a Cyber Sabbath: A full day each week to unplug the computer and fully focus on the faces before me. No e-mail. No writing assignments. Not even one Google. Just rest from cyber world, in the same way God took a day to rest after creating our world.

How could I accomplish this seemingly impossible feat? Planning is the key. I found that it doesn't necessarily have to be on Sunday, but it should be a day that corresponds with the needs and availability of my family. Each Monday, I study my calendar of scheduled events and earmark my Cyber Sabbath for that week.

For writers, e-mail is a life-link to editors, publishers, and agencies essential to our trade. Since most businesses close on weekends, Saturdays or Sundays would be the logical choice as a Cyber Sabbath to avoid missing important career correspondence.

As demanding as Jesus' life was, He still managed to find a quiet place for rest and prayer. And none of us have work that is more important than Jesus'! Our weekly respites, like His, can provide renewed perspective, regeneration of energy, and time to invest in the lives of those most precious to us.

And unlike your kids, it's a sure bet your computer will be there when you get back.

Prayer: *Lord, help me to honor Your directive to observe a day of rest in which to strengthen relationships, regroup, refocus, and refresh—not just in my spiritual life, but my professional life as well. Amen.*

Reflection

Were you surprised to your answer to the quiz or were you aware of the amount of time you spend daily at the computer?

How would you list your top five priorities?

Are you willing to commit to a Cyber Sabbath weekly? If so, pull out your calendar right now and earmark a Cyber Sabbath for next week.

Sunrises and Sunsets

"Don't settle into the lie that it's all up to you. If you do, then you will write for hours with no break. You'll miss sunrises and sunsets. Your faith will be small and your stress level high. Take breaks. Exercise and stretch. Help those who have less than you. You're not just a writer. You're a vessel of the Most High God. When you believe that His yoke is easy and His burden light, you will have faith to take the time to care for your body and your soul." ~Susie Larson, speaker, author of *The Uncommon Woman: Making an Ordinary Life Extraordinary*, www.susielarson.com

Excerpt from "The Downside of Success"

"Our email boxes overflow with notes from those who want our help. Audiences rave about our wisdom or charisma. Some constantly congratulate us for achievements. We become the epitome of their vision of success, and they yearn to connect with us—and to stay connected." ~Cecil Murphey, best-selling author, speaker, and conference teacher, www.themanbehindthewords.com

"Don't put a period where God has a comma, because He has a plan for every life He has created!" ~contributed by Sheri Rose Shepherd, author of *Preparing Him for the Other Woman*, www.hisprincess.com

"Pacing. I'm still learning how to master this. It's so tough. Pacing is all about raising questions the reader wants answered, then giving them an answer just as you raise another question. Sometimes, as a writer and believer, I wonder why God doesn't seem to come through when I want Him to—and then I think of the pacing of my life, of my story, and I see over and over again that He is the best Author of all if I will only trust His story in me." ~Eric Wilson, author of *Field of Blood*, www.wilsonwriter.com

"Some obstacles can be ironed out as they occur and many of the problems we anticipate never happen. So when most circumstances point toward success, make your move. Go for it." ~Mary E. Trimble, author of *Rosemount* and *McClellan's Bluff*, www.whidbey.com/marytrimble

Slow, But Never Late

Suzanne Woods Fisher

"Be still before the Lord and wait patiently for Him, do not fret" (Psalm 37:7, NIV).

Does God ever seem slow to you? Do you ever feel He has a fondness for showing up at the eleventh hour of a crisis? With not a minute to spare?

I do. I call Him the "just-in-time God." There have been many instances in my life when God shows up at the last moment with an unforeseen solution to a problem or by opening a door that had seemed locked shut. Often, He smoothes out a path that I hadn't even considered taking. He always surprises me but never fails me. And yet, when faced with an important issue that needs resolution, whether it's a family emergency or a professional concern, I forget all of that. Waiting seems hard. I just don't like it.

What other career, besides writing, does waiting play such a leading role? Waiting for a response to a query. Then waiting to hear back about a requested manuscript. And finally, waiting to find out if an agent accepts our work after showing a spark of interest.

I used to think that once I was actually contracted to an agent, the wait for publication would get easier. I could relinquish my impatience at apparent inactivity.

Not true. And if I focus on waiting too much, I feel restless. Anxious. Fretful. Eager for a conclusion, even if it's not the right one. Not unlike that path the Israelites took 3000 years ago. They, too, had trouble with waiting and sought a conclusion. A tragic one.

During the forty days in which Moses was up on Mount Sinai with God, the Israelites became anxious and restless. "When the people saw that Moses was so long in coming down from the mountain, they gathered around Aaron and said, 'Come, make us gods who will go before us. As for this fellow Moses who brought us up out of Egypt, we don't know what has happened to him'" (Exodus 32:1).

You know the rest. Aaron complied and made a golden calf for the Israelites to worship. God gave Moses the heads-up to get down the mountain but fast. "When Moses approached the camp and saw the calf and the dancing, his anger burned and he threw the tablets out of his hands, breaking them into pieces at the foot of the mountain" (Exodus 32:19).

The wait overwhelmed them. Those foolish Israelites assumed that apparent inactivity on God's part meant impotence. But here's the part that really *haunts* me: the exact opposite was true. God was delivering the Law to Moses. He was handcrafting the stone tablets to provide structure and peace within their society. He was teaching Moses how to worship. He was tenderly caring and providing for the Israelites' future.

Think how differently this situation could have turned out had the Israelites waited patiently, expectantly, faithfully. Odd to think that in their anxiety, they had a desire to connect with...*something* greater than themselves. What if they had had taken the "wait" and substituted it with "worship?" Imagine if their attitude had been the same as the writer of Lamentations: "In this stillness, I wait, Sovereign God. It is good to wait quietly for you." (Lamentations 3:26, TLB).

Think how differently situations could turn out in our *own* life if we could only wait quietly for God. If we used times of waiting—for a query letter to be answered or for an editor to respond —as *reminders* to worship God? When I do, my prayer life expands, spilling benefits into my work. When I don't, it becomes very tempting to substitute God with a modern day version of a Golden Calf, say, for example, a book deal or an article acceptance. Yes, those goals *can* become Golden Calves if they become the object of our focus.

Do you ever feel as if inactivity on God's part equals impotence? Join me in trying to learn from the mistakes of those impatient, faithless Israelites and not repeat them.

During periods of apparent inactivity God may be preparing a wonderful opportunity for you in your writing career. Who knows what is going on behind the scenes? All that we really know is that our work is committed to Him and that includes its outcome. Never forget that God is working on your behalf.

Prayer: *Sovereign God, I'm so bad at waiting! And yet, I do believe You are my source of hope in every situation, no matter how in the dark I am. Help me to take this confidence with me into my waiting periods, actively expecting Your blessing in due season. Amen.*

Reflection

Describe a recent time of waiting. How did you feel during the wait? What was the outcome?

What have you learned about God's faithfulness when you have periods of waiting?

Could waiting be another word for worship? If so, how can you use waiting as worship?

"With the Lord a day is like a thousand years, and a thousand years are like a day." (2 Peter 3:8, NIV).

Wait in Stillness

"Do not be afraid of silence in your prayer time. It may be that you are meant to listen, not to speak. So wait before the Lord. Wait in stillness. Wait as David waited when he "sat before the Lord." And in that stillness, assurance will come to you. You will know that you are heard; you will know that your Lord ponders the voice of your humble desires; you will hear quiet words spoken to you yourself, perhaps to your grateful surprise and refreshment." ~Amy Carmichael, missionary to India, (1867-1951)

"A couple of months after I determined God had called me to write, I drove to...hear Sena Jeter Naslund, author of *Ahab's Wife* and professor at the University of Louisville, speak to students from the English classes there. I still felt self-conscious at this new writing venture and spoke almost apologetically to her after her talk.

'I'm a late bloomer,' I said. 'At age 54 I've just begun to write seriously.'

'No, don't apologize,' she said. 'The way you have to look at is that you have accumulated all these life experiences, and now you have something to write. Many writers begin later in life.'

After a brief conversation, on the way out, another attendee reminded me that Laura Ingalls Wilder was in her sixties when she began to write her *Little House* books. I left feeling affirmed, invigorated, and ready to write." ~Karen H. Phillips, freelance writer

"Someone told me this at the beginning of my career: 'Don't get it right, get it written.' Until that point, I had a problem with never finishing anything, because I would rewrite the first three chapters over and over, and then I'd get bored and lose interest. I found that if I write the first draft quickly, without judgment, I can go back later and rewrite. So I don't actually get that creative until the second draft. Then I may take it through five or more drafts before it's ready for publication." ~Terri Blackstock, best-selling author of *Second Chances* and the *Sun Coast Chronicles* series, www.terriblackstock.com

"Write to live, don't live to write, or the life will go out of your stories." ~Michelle Buckman, author of *Maggie Come Lately*, www.michellebuckman.com

I'll Do My Part
Faith Tibbetts McDonald

"As each part does its work." (Ephesians 4:16, NIV).

When the Penn State Nittany Lions play football in State College, Pennsylvania, Beaver Stadium is filled to capacity. About a quarter of the 110,000 fans are current students. For each game the students organize to form a t-shirt mosaic. Some students wear white t-shirts and function as white tiles in the mosaic to form the letters PSU. Students in blue t-shirts sit so they provide a Penn State blue background for the white lettering.

In spring 2007, just after the shootings at Virginia Tech, the Penn State Football team played their annual inter-squad scrimmage. Instead of dressing in Penn State blue and white, spectator students dressed in Virginia Tech burgundy and gold. The burgundy students formed a large VT in the stands. The students intended to send a message to the Virginia Tech students: we are standing with you, and there is hope.

I like that message. It's similar to the message I want to send with my writing. Sometimes, I might alter it slightly to say: God is standing with you, and there is hope. Years of reading have convinced me that a significant chunk of Christian writing is a variation on that theme. That is the gospel in a nutshell, after all.

When I think about how many Christian authors—some really good, best-selling ones—are writing on that theme, I can begin to wonder about the significance my work. If we are all writing to convey the same message, it's probably being broadcast loud and clear, and there is probably no way my contribution, or lack thereof, will be noticed.

I feel like Amos in *Chicago* who sings about the pain of not being noticed. He describes people who are noticed in crowds—those who yell, who wave arms and legs, who excitedly convey urgent messages. In fact, he says, everyone is noticed at sometime or other—most don't even have to act in attention-getting ways. They are noticed. He contrasts this by describing how he gets noticed. Never. He says that his name should have been Mr. Cellophane—people don't see him, they see through him.

Like Amos, I feel invisible. I fear my writing won't matter.

I'm tempted to think that prolific, highly regarded authors like Chuck Swindol (70+ titles to his name) and Max Lucado (dozens of published books) and Anne Graham Lotz (ditto)...well, they matter. But the writing of a nobody like me? It's invisible and inconsequential. Maybe I should go serve soup at the local soup kitchen instead of pouring myself into writing. Or sign up to work in the church nursery.

However, remembering the stadiums' enormous PSU and the giant VT inspires me to continue writing my part. How many students would have to show up dressed in the wrong color before the entire message would become blotchy gibberish? One or two could show up dressed in pink without impact—maybe it would take a hundred or two to render the mosaic indiscernible. But I don't want to be one of those hundred. Do you?

We are writers who along with a mighty crowd, are privileged to declare the good news of a God who loves and who wants to be involved in peoples' lives. There is hope.

Let's do our part to declare that message.

Prayer: *Lord, Help me to write what You've called me to write with my whole heart, mind, and strength. Help me remember that You notice a job well-done. Please let my work have the impact You desire it to have. Amen.*

Reflection

What is the message you've been called to declare with your writing?

When is the last time you felt your work did not matter? How did the Lord encourage you to continue?

Pray for someone you know who may be discouraged thinking their contribution is inconsequential.

"Advice for aspiring writers? Stop! Stop right now! Stop limiting your potential by fear (Go on - submit that piece!), low expectations (if God gave you the assignment to write, He'll use your abilities "beyond anything you can imagine," Eph. 3:20), or lack of energy (*He gives strength to the weary and increases the power of the weak,* Isaiah 40:29.)" - Debora M. Coty, author of *Mom Needs Chocolate: Hugs, Humor and Hope for Surviving Motherhood* www.DeboraCoty.com

"The poet/psalmist spent time with God, and the prophetic verse was written under the inspiration of the Creator of all things. If we then feel the call of God to write for His glory, how shall we expect to accomplish such an awesome task if we do not spend time in His presence and write under the inspiration of the Almighty?" ~Ruth Carmichael Ellinger, author of *The Wild Rose of Lancaster* and *Wild Rose of Promise,* www.ruthellinger.com

"Focus is what gives your story cohesiveness. You must be able to describe your story in on sentence. Yes. One sentence. Forcing this focus gives you a home base to return to and reflect from and ensures that you don't drift too much in other directions." ~Sandy Tritt, author of *Everything I Know,* editor, www.InspirationforWriters.com

Excerpt from "Pushing Through the Pain of Publishing"

"As I prepared to write my first manuscript, I was so distracted during the day that I kept procrastinating. I was under the impression that I'd write whenever I got around to it. But any writer will tell you that you don't *find* time to write. You must *make* time to write." ~ Shannon Etheridge, best-selling author of the *Every Woman's Battle* series and *Loving Jesus Without Limits* series, www.shannonetheridge.com

"Most Christians, like me, view their writing as a ministry, but one day they will realize publishers must view their writing as a business. So if you want to break in, that means you need to make yourself look like a *wise investment*. Every Christian prays that God will make their book succeed! What sets your book proposal apart from other Christians who are praying for the same thing?" ~Gary Thomas, author of *Sacred Marriage*, www.garythomas.com

Rock Collecting

Joanna Bloss

"Each of you is to take up a stone on his shoulder...to serve as a sign among you...These stones are to be a memorial for the people of Israel forever" (Joshua 4:7, NIV).

My ten-year-old son is a rock collector. His collection wouldn't exactly garner a place in the E-bay sales hall of fame, nor would it do much to impress an avid rock hound. However, it is priceless—at least to my son. The value of the collection is not in the rocks—most were picked up on fishing trips with Dad or on the school playground—it's largely sentimental. As every ten-year-old boy who collects rocks knows, the value is in what the rocks *mean*, the memories they represent.

God encourages rock collecting, too. He uses them to help us remember significant events.

He often instructed the children of Israel to build altars out of rocks to remember how He answered their prayers for deliverance. I can imagine them naming these piles of rocks *The Lord Will Provide* or *God is Faithful*. Mere rocks became holy altars because of the memories attached to them and the meaning they held.

Remembering is important not only because it gives meaning to our past, but because it gives motivation for our present and hope for our future. I've found this to be true in my life, both spiritually and practically. I accidentally stumbled on this truth one day when I discovered that remembering serves a very distinct purpose in my writing.

Years ago God impressed upon me the desire to communicate with words. Sometimes desire alone is enough to keep me putting fingers to the keyboard. But there are days when time is fleeting, words are scarce, and rejections are many. On those days, I have trouble remembering why I write. I doubt the fact that God has called me to write. I get discouraged. I want to give up. I ask myself: Why on earth am I chaining myself to a computer when it all seems so futile?

Not long ago, I was battling this feeling. I had just about decided to give up completely when I happened to sift through some files in my office. Among the rejection letters and tax receipts was a little pile of writing mementos: a copy of my very first writing paycheck, a yellowed newspaper column by the late Erma Bombeck, a note from someone who was encouraged by one of my articles, a stack of magazines with articles with my byline. These once forgotten items gave me a jolt and radically changed my perspective of despair.

I discovered that keeping these things served a far greater purpose than mere sentiment. Like the altar rocks of Israel, three particular "rocks of remembrance" helped me recall why I wanted to write in the first place and gave me needed inspiration to continue.

Remembering gave *meaning to my past.* One of my first published articles was about helping my older children grieve when I suffered a miscarriage. A few weeks after the article was published, the editor sent me a stack of e-mails she'd received in response. Reading those e-mails reminded me of how God used a painful experience to make a difference in the lives of others. Maybe my words really did matter!

Remembering gave me *motivation for the present.* The Erma Bombeck column I saved is called "If You Want to Write Just Do It." It was about eliminating excuses to make writing a reality instead of a dream. I smiled when I remembered how this column initially inspired me.

Finally, remembering gave me *hope for my future.* God often instructed the Israelites to tell of His mighty deeds to their children and their children's children. Why? Because if God was faithful in the past, He will most certainly be in the future. Those rejections might have piled up on my desk, but if God could use one of my articles two years ago to encourage a family, He could certainly do it two years from now.

As long as I keep writing!

How has God proved Himself faithful in your writing career? Whether or not you consider yourself sentimental, I encourage you to begin collecting a few "rocks" of your own. Save them and put them aside where you'll be sure to find them on one of those days in which you need a healthy dose of inspiration.

Hopefully, like me, you'll find enormous value in your little pile of stones. I suppose my tattered collection of writing mementos has no physical value, but that doesn't change the fact that they are worth keeping. After all, to me and to God, they're priceless.

Prayer: *Father, You have called me to write and have been faithful to help me accomplish every task You've asked me to do. But I often forget. Help me to find meaningful and creative ways to remember Your faithfulness to me. Amen.*

Reflection

Have you saved any mementos since starting your writing career? If so, list some of the items that are meaningful to you.

How, specifically, has God affirmed your desire to be a writer?

Take a moment to gather some tangible reminders of God's call on your life. Consider putting them in a special place (maybe in a keepsake box?) so that on days when you need it, you'll be able to find inspiration from the memories they evoke.

If You Want to Write

"If you are one of the many writers on the long ambitious path, what do you do? First you keep growing and working at your craft. If you want to write books, then learn how to write an excellent book proposal. If you are trying to get an agent or publisher, learn how to write a great query letter. Every day I see countless, forgettable queries. You want to write one which stands out. Get to a writer's conference and begin to connect with other writers and editors." ~Terry Whalin, agent, Whalin Literary Agency

Time Management 101 for Writers

1. Lower your standards for household chores.
2. Delegate.
3. Ban television from your life.
4. Add a few good, nutritious fast foods and convenience foods to your weekly menu.
5. Multi-task.
6. Practice the art of "just say no."
   ~Deborah Raney, author of *A Vow to Cherish*,
www.deborahraney.com

"Technology can be a blessing and a curse. With the ease of chatting online, researching, and zipping off queries and pleas for help, writers can find themselves spending far too much time in front of the computer and not enough time with family and friends or completing 'other' tasks. When my income level dropped, I realized that while I had been in front of a computer for 10 to 12 hours a day, I wasn't using that time productively." ~ Alyice Edrich, author, editor, *The Dabbling Mum*®, website, www.thedabblingmum.com

"Work through your fears. I was having a terrible time with marketing my book until I stopped and analyzed the fear that was stopping me. Once I reasoned through my childhood fear from an adult perspective, I've been bold as a lion in marketing myself and my book." ~Debra L. Butterfield, author of *Help! My Husband Has Sexually Abused Our Daughter*, www.debralbutterfield.com

"I know an editor who has this sign in his office: 'We don't reject writers. We reject pieces of paper with writing on them.' A great lesson there. Never take rejection personally. If you do, you'll never survive in this business." ~Tom Neven, author of *Do Fish Know They're Wet?* and *On the Frontline*, www.tomneven.com

Interruptions!

Suzanne Woods Fisher

"When Jesus heard what had happened, He withdrew by boat privately to a solitary place. Hearing of this, the crowds followed Him on foot from the towns. When Jesus landed and saw a large crowd, He had compassion on them and healed their sick" (Matthew 14:13-14, NIV).

A typical morning: By 8:30 a.m., I had taken a shower, started coffee, fed the dogs, roused my kids, read a short piece of Scripture, checked e-mail, made school lunches, given another wake up call to my son, replied to some e-mails, whipped on a modest amount of make-up, made the bed, double-checked to make sure everyone had breakfast and brushed their teeth, replied to one more e-mail, hustled the kids into the car, dropped them off at school, stopped at the grocery store to get a few things for dinner, bumped into a friend which slowed down my shopping, zoomed home, unloaded groceries, and finally, *finally* sat down to write.

Ah! My favorite moment of the morning. The house was blessedly still, and my mind was free.

And *then* the phone rang. Glancing at caller I.D., I sighed, knowing I needed to take this call. It was from someone I loved with a pressing need.

Jesus' daily life was riddled with interruptions. On His way somewhere, to go do something, He would be stopped by a hopeful rich young ruler, by a heartbroken father, by a wily Pharisee. He was so approachable that children scrambled to get on His lap.

How did He manage? How did He keep his thoughts on track? Able to focus when He needed to focus, and yet shift His attentions, so masterfully, to soul-sick individuals? Almost as if He was expecting them. Granted, Jesus was the son of God. He had an eternal perspective on His days that I can barely grapple to understand.

Still, His life is our model. There's something important to glean about Jesus' response to interruptions, even beyond seeing them as divine appointments. As long as our focus remains fixed on God, interruptions may work to our benefit.

Let's take the ideal day of a writer: Long, quiet hours "in the zone" when our minds concentrate intently, our bodies are hunched over a keyboard. Ideal? Well, not really.

Physiologically, our bodies must move. Some computer software "pings" every fifteen minutes to remind the user to get up and stretch. Our hands, arms, and shoulders need to be relieved of the typing task to avoid repetitive injuries. Our backs will take on the shape of a question mark if they aren't frequently straightened.

And mentally? Our minds need to stretch, too. They need fresh air, sunlight, cobwebs swept out so there is room for a pause, to reconsider options, for new ideas to germinate.

In the middle of an article recently, I was interrupted for a few days with a family emergency. By the time I was able to return to my work, I had stumbled on some information that would change direction for the article, significantly improving it. That lesson taught me that God can make use of an interruption, in that case, by providing me with information that I needed. He is sovereign in our lives even over interruptions.

In his gospel, Mark noted that Jesus was often praying *when* He was interrupted. If we can assume that Jesus' priorities for the day were established *through* prayer, then it is reasonable to conclude interruptions to His day's work *was* His day's work or at least a part of it.

There's a lesson in that. My days needed rearranging. First priority: valuable, prayerful time with the Lord so that I don't get spiritually undernourished. That includes relinquishing my day to Him. Second priority: loving those whom God has put in my path today. Third priority: writing well.

So today, I woke up a little earlier. Got the coffee going, fed the dog, checked my e-mail, and then sat down for a half of an hour with my Bible. I even had a few extra minutes for prayer for all this new day will hold. I have a hunch that, today, my writing will improve.

Prayer: *Lord Jesus, I need a critical shift of viewpoint about how my day unfolds. Help me to lay aside my brittle expectations and hand my to-do list over to You. I give this day to You, knowing You will go before me into every choice, every encounter, every opportunity. Amen.*

Reflection

How do interruptions affect you?

Instead of letting your schedule hold you captive, is there a way you can build a margin into your day to allow for God's interruptions?

"Don't wait for the perfect time to write. Don't use the excuse that your household is too busy and that if you could just get away to a quiet spot you'd write a best-seller. Most successful authors I know write wherever, whenever. With children running circles around them. In airports, on planes, and in the car between pick-ups. And don't wait for your crisis of the moment to be over. It's been in the worst of times I've written my best stuff, (yes, even humor) when I was frantic and my emotions were closest to the surface. Go figure!" ~Sue Buchanan, humorist, author of *The Bigger the Hair, the Closer to God,* www.suebue.com

"God knows the plan for today. Sometimes it involves writing, and other times it doesn't. There are mornings when I seek God, and I clearly hear, 'Writing will not happen today, don't stress.' This gentle voice is always right. There will be family needs or young moms that I need to minister to. This is part of God's plan, too. Being obedient to Christ moment by moment is far more difficult than sitting down and pounding out a 300-page novel, but obedience is always the better way." ~Tricia Goyer, author of *Life Interrupted,* www.triciagoyer.com

Top Ten Things I've Learned as a Writer:

10. Not every other Christian writer is nice—but not every editor is mean, either.

9. My children's desire to "hold you, mommy" increases as my deadline nears.

8. My desire for my own mommy increases as my deadline nears.

7. Fellow writers are the coolest people on the planet...at least most of them.

6. Writers' conferences are refreshing and exhausting at the same time.

5. Getting a book contract makes you feel like a "real writer"...for the first five minutes.

4. Rejection and waiting to hear about submissions does not get any easier.

3. Finding a good agent is harder than finding a good publisher.

2. Finding a good publisher is getting more and more difficult if you don't have big sales numbers.

1. Even with all the difficult aspects of writing, I still wouldn't trade my job for anything. I get to play with words all day—in my PJ's, if I want to! ~Dena Dyer, author of *The Groovy Chicks Road Trip to Love*, http://denadyer.typepad.com

"Write out of a concern to help others." ~Dr. Gary D. Chapman, Ph.D., best-selling author of *The Five Love Languages*, www.garychapman.org

Who's Your Daddy?

Debora M. Coty

"Look at the birds. They don't need to plant or harvest or put food in barns because your heavenly Father feeds them. And you are far more valuable to him than they are" (Matthew 6:26, NLT).

I was standing in the grocery store deli line waiting to place my order for a half pound each of smoked turkey and baby Swiss. I read all the signs on the counter. Twice. After babbling incoherently to the baby in the stroller beside me, I counted floor tiles. I studied the designer outfit and three inch stiletto heels of the lady in front of me and convinced myself that she was probably coveting my jeans and sneakers about now.

My eyes lit on a book in the small inspirational book rounder by the pizza crusts. Comprehension slowly sank in. I felt my eyeballs bulge out of their sockets.

Right there, wedged between King James and Billy Graham, was a book amazingly similar to the one I'd just written—identical theme, near-same title, word length within ten pages, same publisher I'd just been rejected by (guess that's why!), and as I flipped to the acknowledgments, I found that the author and I even shared the same agent. Only she'd sold 30,000 copies and I had yet to receive an e-mail reply.

There seemed to be something smelly in the deli besides the Limburger.

When I got home with my lunchmeat and book du jour, I began digging for clues. It became painfully clear to me that King Solomon was right: there are no new ideas under the sun. The author and I apparently shared many of the same viewpoints, and she beat me to the punch in writing them down.

But surely my book was just as good! Wasn't it?

As I devoured the first three chapters with the goal of comparing books, a hot poker stabbed my pride. Hers was better. Her word pictures were sharper, anecdotes funnier, and take-away's more succinct.

Dark tentacles of inferiority began creeping upward from their deeply buried casket within my innards. *No! No, I will not allow Satan to paralyze me with self-doubt again!* I thought I had learned that lesson after a recent struggle with writing insecurity that stifled all creativity and effectively halted production. Some call it writer's block. I call it spiritual gridlock.

"Lord," I prayed, "I can't go there again. Inferiority is a merciless, cold-blooded beast that swallows me whole and then spits me out in chewed-up, indigestible pieces. Please rescue me!"

As I sat glued to my chair waiting for God's miraculous lightning bolt of intervention, a still, small thought implanted itself in my frantic brain. At first I wasn't sure if I was rehashing song lyrics I'd recently heard from my teenager's radio or if it was a communication wave from a higher tower. The message was simple, but profound.

"Who's your Daddy?"

"Um...are you talking to me, Lord?"

"Who's your Daddy?"

My first response was concrete. "My dad is Frank Mitchell, of course—the gentle, godly man who is always there for me, who understands me and loves me unconditionally. The benevolent provider who takes care of his little girl."

"But who's your *Daddy*?"

"Oh. Why, you're my Heavenly Father, my Abba, my spiritual Daddy."

And suddenly I got it. All those attributes that belonged to my earthly father applied even more to my heavenly Father. He will always be there for me, understand me, and love me unconditionally. He will provide for me in ways I cannot comprehend.

Who am I trying to please, anyway?

As I pulled my Heavenly Daddy's warm, snug blanket of security around me, I felt my inner turmoil relax. God gave me my talents and abilities. He made me just the way I am, knowing precisely how He would use my writing gift to best glorify Him. If I'm not "good enough" in someone else's eyes—or heaven forbid, my own eyes— it's my creator's responsibility, not mine. My job is only to do the best I can with what I've been allocated by my Heavenly Father. The rest is up to Him.

I recall recently listening to an audio tape of my now twenty-four-year-old son as he sang a very off-key rendition of *Jesus Loves Me* at age three. In the opinion of most people, his skills would be considered rudimentary, even lacking. But I was deeply touched by the most beautiful voice on the planet, blessed and proud as only a parent can be. I taught him that song, and he was doing his part to learn and improve.

And that's exactly the way God, our heavenly parent, views our writing skills. He taught us everything we know, through avenues of formal education, experience, and aptitude. Now it's up to us to continue learning and improving. He even fabricated our hearts—that mysterious motivational place within us that drives us to share through the written word His joy, His work in our lives, His hope with others.

If we view our writing careers through the Daddy filter, the pressure of being "good enough" is lifted. Our Heavenly Father will be blessed and proud of our accomplishments on any level. And we'll *know* who our Daddy is!

Prayer: *Abba, Father (Heavenly Daddy), help us remember that You are the One we're trying to please and that the journey to accomplishment is part of Your gift to us. Amen.*

Reflection

Cite a recent time when Satan paralyzed your writing productivity with self-doubt.

How did God work you through it?

What are three ways your Heavenly Daddy taught you everything you know about writing?

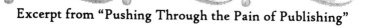

Excerpt from "Pushing Through the Pain of Publishing"

"I posted a sheet of paper above my computer with the following words penned by T.D. Jakes in *The Lady, Her Lover, Her Lord:*

'God has a plan for you. If you lose your optimism, the enemy has won. Place your hope with the power of God. Place your future in the hands of God. Don't you know that God had something special in mind when He made you? He had a specific role that only you can play. Refuse to forfeit His plan just because of your pain. Bear it like a woman in labor. Know that the pain will pass, and the promise will be delivered...This is no time to faint now, dear lady. Grab the sides of the bed and push!'" ~ Shannon Etheridge, author of the *Every Woman's Battle* series and the *Loving Jesus Without Limits* series, www.shannonetheridge.com

"When I first started in the writing, speaking, and media business, I had nineteen out of every twenty doors slam shut. Now, I'm 'successful' because I only have nine out of ten doors shut in my face!" ~Ellie Kay, America's Family Financial Expert®, best-selling author of eleven books, www.elliekay.com

"Research does more than add authenticity—it often opens the door to subplots and additional scenes." ~Sandy Tritt, author of *Everything I Know*, editor, www.InspirationForWriters.com

Words, Words, Words

"Words are important. They either clarify or cloud your purpose. Changing them does one or the other, so know which by cultivating a strong sense of your work and purpose in writing." ~Mick Silva, editor, Waterbrook Press

"Be patient. Most new books will take two to three years from conception to bookshelf. It is a long process with a lot of stops and starts." ~Trish Berg, author of *Rattled* and *The Great American Supper Swap,* www.trishberg.com

Inspired Ideas

Faith Tibbetts McDonald

"My heart is stirred by a noble theme..." (Psalm 45:1, NIV).

One day on a New York City sidewalk I overheard a woman talking with a successful exhibiting artist. The spectator confided that she was studying art at a prestigious art school and hoped to make her mark in the art world.

Unimpressed by the *impressive* school, the artist offered an alternate basis for predictions of success: "When they see your work, does anyone say 'Aha!'?"

Like artists, writers yearn to produce inspired work; work that prompts an audience to burst out with a spontaneous "Aha!"

To write an inspired piece, we must find a stirring idea. However, finding and recognizing an inspired idea is not always easy. Sometimes, I wake in the night with an idea for a book or article that is so stirring, so brilliant, so obviously the beginnings of a poignant piece that I pry myself out of bed, grope in the dark for a pen and paper, and record the idea.

Inevitably, in the morning when I review the idea—after coffee—I find that my nighttime judgment is skewed. The idea is tossed into the wastebasket.

For me, writing ideas are best prompted by conversations, observations, or reading. Or they occur when I'm exercising or gazing out the window as I sit at the computer.

As I tell my college students, *first* ideas are not always *best* ideas. Writers must allow an idea time to develop. Sometimes, the ideas that wake me in the night are the seeds that—through prayer—grow into a stirring piece.

As an idea develops, I've learned to ask questions to discern its potential: Am I qualified to write on this subject? Do I know, or can I learn, enough to write a worthwhile piece? But most of all: does this subject stir my heart?

I think that inspired ideas begin in the heart of God. Once He stirs our hearts with an idea, we must strive to express it in apt words. We must find words that stir readers' hearts like Peter's at Pentecost: confident, filled with truth, powerful to do God's work (Acts 2). Like Philip's to the Ethiopian eunuch: right on time (Acts 8: 26-39). Like Paul's: sometimes encouraging, sometimes exhorting. Like Jesus': filled with compassion and graced with wit.

Modern writers, while not writing words that are God-breathed and error-free like those recorded in Scripture, write words that are eloquent and inspiring. Joni Eareckson Tada's words resonate with truth far beyond my experience and compel me to reach for truth. T. S. Eliot's words tell memorably of a mystery so wonderful I ache to know it. Calvin Miller's poems rekindle my love for Jesus.

Like these authors, we can—and should—strive for eloquence in our writing. Inspiration, however, does not always accompany eloquence and striving. To write inspired words, we must write with a certain amount of forgetting ourselves.

Most often, I've found that the words I have written that compel readers are not the ones that were painstakingly alliterated and meticulously selected. When a reader claims that she read my piece and it touched her heart, almost always I think, "I said that?"

Inspiration—the Aha!—comes when God writes through us. Throughout time, God has selected people like us to make His ideas visible. According to the book of Exodus, He selected craftsmen to implement His creative ideas in the tabernacle. The craftsmen He selected were willing, able and skilled (Exodus 35:31). With meticulous attention to detail, they fashioned valuable raw materials into an exquisite, furnished dwelling to house God's Spirit on earth. People could go meet Him there.

Words are writers' raw material. With attention to detail, like word order and punctuation, writers arrange words to tell a moving story or convey a message. We willingly use our skills and abilities in hopes that the Holy Spirit will live in our words. Then our words will jump off the paper. They will prompt an "Aha!" They will complete God's work in readers' hearts.

Prayer: *Lord, please make me skilled, willing, and able to write as You have called me to. Holy Spirit, please fill these words I write with You. Amen.*

Reflection

List ways to find writing ideas: read newspapers, watch Oprah, observe surroundings etc.

What ideas pique your interest? What angle interests you most? What genre of writing inspires you?

What can you do to allow more room for inspiration in your work?

Scientists have discovered that a breakthrough idea is not a one-time event. They have identified a series of four stages in formation of an idea:

- Preparation stage: be open to and actively consider new ideas.
- Incubation stage: wait. The subconscious mind is working.
- The "Aha!"
- Verification: test the idea out on others and see if they agree it has merit.

Check out Christian Classics at http://www.ccel.org These inspired ideas became manuscripts that have lasted hundreds of years.

"A great title is a beginning, your very best writing is a necessity, but unless people know it's in the store, all that effort is for naught. Publishers are now looking for marketing 'partners' – authors who will work with them to launch a book into the marketplace. That could include everything from doing radio and print interviews to mailing or emailing your potential readers to doing signings at local bookstores to posting your books on a website." ~Liz Curtis Higgs, author of 26 books, including the best-selling *Bad Girls of the Bible* series, www.lizcurtishiggs.com

Excerpt from *The Downside of Success*

"Because our readers touch our needy, unhealed parts, we're seduced by the attention. Our feelings about ourselves become inflated. We worry about our image or what people think of us. Instead, we need to realize that fame and attention stir up unresolved issues within ourselves." ~Cecil Murphey, best-selling author, speaker, and conference teacher, www.themanbehindthewords.com

"Just as you must not believe the effusive praise of your inner circle, you should not accept the criticism of strangers without evaluating it against the learning you've acquired while applying your high respect for your gift and calling."
~Mick Silva, editor, Waterbrook Press

The Manuscript is Perfect! We'll Change *Everything!*

Suzanne Woods Fisher

"Let us not become weary in doing good, for at the proper time we will reap a harvest if we do not give up" (Galatians 6:9, NIV).

In the movie *Father of the Bride*, Martin Short, who plays the flamboyant foreign wedding planner, admires the front of Steve Martin's house, scrutinizing the layout for the upcoming wedding and reception. "I *love* it! It's *perfect!*" he gushes. Then he turns to his assistant. "We change *everything*," he whispers.

In a snapshot, *that's the writer's life.* We send in our best work—our heart and soul—and the editor loves it, but wants to change everything.

Writing is very personal. When I send off work to a publisher, it feels as if I'm standing in front of the world in my underwear. My interior pose is exposed through the written word, acutely vulnerable, open for comment by the powers that be. More often than not, those comments include criticism, the need to re-write, and a Goliath-sized amount of rejection.

And *that's* why God has a soft spot for writers. He understands vulnerability.

Long ago, the prophet Samuel had devoted his life as the liaison between the developing nation of Israel and the Lord. He was good at it, too. "Throughout Samuel's lifetime, the hand of the Lord was against the Philistines" (1 Samuel 7:13).

When Samuel grew old, the Israelites decided they were ready for a leadership change and dismissed Samuel's wayward sons as potential successors. Israel clamored for a king so they could be like the other nations. Samuel was displeased, "so he prayed to the Lord. And the Lord told him: 'Listen to all that the people are saying to you; it is not you they have rejected but they have rejected me as their king'" (1 Samuel 8:6-7).

Catch that? Samuel was handed a very personal, terribly disappointing rejection, and he responded by *praying.* He didn't deny his hurt feelings but took them straight to the Lord for resolution. God's tender response enabled Samuel to see the big picture and to understand that this issue wasn't really about him.

We writerly types often need a similar change in viewpoint, one that keeps the big picture in clear view. We need to develop a resilient response to editing or rejection so that we don't become easily derailed and sink into discouragement. True, there are editors who rebuff coldly, leaving the writer with a vague sense of failure. But the bulk of rejection letters are usually written because the work isn't directed to the right venue. *Handmaiden* editor Virginia Nieuwsma admits, "I regularly reject good manuscripts with merit that just don't fit what we are looking for."

And then there are the editors who chop up a writer's work so that it is unrecognizable or poorly edited. It happens. Wince and then develop calluses. Step back and consider the big picture. Let it go and move on to a new project.

When editors want to change or even reject my work, it helps to remember that it might not be about me. They are getting paid to make decisions in the best interests of their company. Rejection doesn't have to become a destructive and personal issue. By asking for constructive feedback, I've received suggestions from editors to improve a manuscript—and most often, they're right. The end result *is* better. And isn't that the point?

Editing, revising, rejecting our work—it can feel personal, but try not to go there. Instead, pray about it. Like Samuel, give those feelings of disappointment to God to resolve. Samuel's work didn't end when Israel anointed its king. Our work shouldn't end because of an editors' negative response. And most importantly, don't stop writing.

Prayer: *Today, Lord, I just have to pour out my heart. This writing gig is too hard! Help me to not grow weary, despite editor's critical comments, despite more rejection. You have promised that my efforts will bring results, so teach me to look expectantly for Your blessings. Amen.*

Reflection

How do you feel when someone edits your work?

Are you developing calluses from rejection? Does it still take as long to rebound as it did a year ago? If not, why not?

What steps can you take to improve your response?

"Be open to the changes an editor may suggest. Consider her a key team member who's helping you become a better communicator of the story you long to tell. Remember, there's nothing sacred about your words, so don't balk at suggestions to reorganize your material, or to add anecdotes, or to 'show, rather than tell' Even the best writers benefit from great editors—and together, you see yourself grow in your ability to write for God's glory and his kingdom." ~Jane Johnson Struck, former editor, "Today's Christian Woman" magazine, and former editor to "MomSense" magazine.

"Many aspiring writers feel like Moses facing the promised land: It's too big. It's too scary. I can't go in there! But God *prepared* the promised land for Israel. The ten spies looked at it as if they were on their own." - Debora M. Coty, author of *The Distant Shore* and *Billowing Sails* www.DeboraCoty.com

"Father, teach me how to glorify you
with each stroke of the pen,
every click of the keyboard,
that your great harvest may come in."
~Sally Jadlow, author of *The Late Sooner*,
www.sallyjadlow.com

"I have made this longer because I have not had the time to make it shorter." ~Blaise Pascal, submitted by Jennie Hilligus, contributor to *A Cup of Comfort: Book of Prayer*

"In the midst of the craziness of the publishing world, never forget that you were called into it by a God who loves you enough to write your story. As long as He's the author of your every breath, you need not worry about the outcome." ~Rebeca Seitz, President, Glass Road Public Relations, LLC

Excavating Ethics

Debora M. Coty

"You shall not steal" (Exodus 20:15, NIV).

No way! How could it be? I couldn't believe my eyes. There on my computer screen, mass e-mailed to me like dozens of other "motivational" messages daily, was an excerpt from one of my published articles, incorporated into a compilation of "cute stories" meant to lift the reader's spirits.

No credit. No names. No authorization. My plagiarized words glared back at me like a sizzling warning flare.

The article had only appeared in my newspaper column (with my byline and picture) and in the "published works" section of my website. The thief must have known who wrote it. What was to prevent this unscrupulous person from returning to the scene of the heist to help himself to more of my hard work?

I felt violated. Helpless. With no way of tracing the culprit, I had no recourse except to pray that it didn't happen again.

My indignation simmered as I realized a stranger had robbed me of the opportunity to use my own anecdote—a true story that happened to my little girl—in the book I'm currently writing. It would no longer be fresh and effective after making the rounds of millions of home computers as an anonymous tale.

I fear that the general public and we writers are woefully uneducated about copyright infringements. Amy Cook, Writer's Digest legal expert, states that "Original stories, poems and quotes are all copyrighted materials, whether they exist on a piece of paper or a computer screen. If you don't get permission from the people who hold the rights, then you're stealing their material."[1]

Unfortunately, plagiarism lives and breathes in the professional writing world. In recent years, Kaavya Viswanathan's novel, *How Opal Mehta Got Kissed, Got Wild, and Got a Life* was yanked from bookshelves, and her six-figure publishing contract was rescinded when it was disclosed that she'd pilfered material from books by Megan McCafferty.[2]

Other writers of note have also admitted to "borrowing" excerpts from fellow writers, for example Doris Kearns Goodwin, who excerpted passages verbatim from author Lynn McTaggart's non-fiction book on Kathleen Kennedy.[2] Dan Brown, author of *The Da Vinci Code* is still selling books despite multiple accusations of plagiarism leveled at him.

Writers new to the field need to make themselves aware of the pitfalls and dangers of sloppy literary license. We may steal rights without even realizing it. Christians, in keeping with our goal to lead others to Christ by our living example, should hold the bar high in the realm of moral standards.

"We put no stumbling block in anyone's path, so that our ministry will not be discredited" (2 Corinthians 6:3, NIV).

We must take care to use organizations' logos or trademarks properly. For example, Xerox® and Velcro® brand hook and loop fasteners are registered trademarks with specific usage guidelines and should be used only as capitalized adjectives to identify the company's products and services, never as verbs ("Please xerox that article," or "Why don't you velcro that shoe?").[3] Terms like Google and Netflix are beginning to be used generically, but caution should be taken with these and other descriptive trademarked words like Frisbee, Cineplex, and La-Z-Boy.

Written material on the Web is not considered public domain. Using a reasonably sized quote is acceptable, but the source must be cited. Even paraphrased thoughts should include attribution so that the reader is not deceived into believing the thought is original.[4]

So how do writers legally and ethically glean ideas from published material?

The U.S. Copyright Office says, "You may make a new claim in your work if the changes are substantial and creative—something more than just editorial changes or minor changes." That includes your own work for which you've sold "all rights." Amy Cook states, "An all-rights contract means that the writer no longer has the ability to sell that article elsewhere, unlike if you sold only first rights" (which generally means you retain rights to resell your work after its first publication).

Cook continues, "Since ideas cannot be copyrighted, you are certainly free to use the same idea, but you must approach it differently...from another point of view or target a different audience."[5]

We can personalize ideas from magazine and newspaper articles, press releases, favorite old books, tall tales, family jokes, church bulletins, even meaningful letters (altering names, of course). I've used the same basic material, recycled and revamped for a women's magazine, a general population newspaper, a national writing trade magazine, and a young mother's seminar.

Contrary to popular belief, book titles and character names can't be copyrighted. However, if the title or name is "distinctive" enough to be associated with a preexisting work, trademark laws may apply. To be safe, stay away from highly recognizable monikers. For example, you could build your book around a character named Prissie, but you might reconsider calling your novel *Gone with the Wind* or naming your protagonist Scarlet O'Hara.

We don't need to steal! Ideas are everywhere—they just need our fresh approach to become morally and legally ours.

Prayer: *Master Creator, teach me the right way—Your way—to create word images that reflect Your nature. Convict me to be upright and honest in all my writing endeavors. Amen.*

[1] Quotation by Amy Cook, *Writer's Digest*, March 2004 Issue, "Questions and Quandaries" by Brian A Klems, p.24.

[2] *Writer's Digest*, October 2006 issue, "The Age of Embellishment" by Tom Conner, p. 27-28.

[3] *Writer's Digest*, September 1998 issue, "Trademark Troubles" by Frank Sennett, p. 51-53.

[4] *Writer's Digest*, May 2006 issue, "Are You An Ethical Writer?" by Donna G. Albrecht, p. 48.

[5] *Writer's Digest,* August 2003 issue, "Ask the Lawyer" by Amy Cook, attorney and literary agent, p. 54.

Reflection

Are there any ways I may be using copyrighted material illegally without really considering it a sin?

As a Christian, am I holding the bar high enough in the realm of moral standards to avoid being a stumbling block to others watching me?

Brainstorm ways to parlay one of your ideas into articles or stories for three different publications.

To research which trademarked words are legally restricted, visit the INTA: International Trademark Association (inta.org)

Just What *Is* a Pseudonym?

A pseudonym is a pen name, a fictitious name, used by an author for publication. For example, Samuel Clemens chose the name "Mark Twain" because it was a term used on riverboats. Pseudonyms are trademarked and are registered with the U.S. Patent & Trademark Office at 800-782-9199.

"Conflict. John LeCarre says that 'The dog sat on the mat' is not a story, while 'The dog sat on the cat's mat' is full of potential. We all deal with conflict in daily life, from the mundane issues of getting hair to cooperate, to the deep issues of a marriage on the brink. Without conflict, a story drags and, even worse, slips into lazy idealism. Jesus and His nature come through a story best when we are truthful in painting the murky reality of life, the very reality into which He immersed Himself on our behalf." ~Eric Wilson, author of *Facing the Giants*, www.wilsonwriter.com

Advice to Myself

"your terrain is full of them

enthusiastic yellow words
whistle a blissful tune

scarlet syllables
wave and shout

murky umber characters
scurry silently

lush jade verbs
labor without direction

orange adjectives
streak through the grass

black fonts
lounge on lawn chairs

grab them
tame them
employ them

compose a story"

~Arlene Knickerbocker, © 2004, author, editor, teacher, author of *Open the Door to Another Realm*

Section 3: I Give Up! Too Many Rejections!

"More than anything else, keep working at the journey. For most of us, it is long and more like a marathon than a short sprint." ~Terry Whalin, agent, Whalin Literary Agency

"Waiting is the publishing world's way of saying, 'Get busy on your next project.'" ~Alton Gansky, author of *Finder's Fee*, www.altongansky.com

I See the Wind and Start to Sink
Suzanne Woods Fisher

"And when they climbed into the boat, the wind died down.

Then those who were in the boat worshiped him, saying, 'Truly you are the Son of God'" (Matthew 14:32-33, NIV).

After a long day facing hungry, needy crowds, Jesus sent the disciples off in a boat and told them He would meet them later on the other side of the lake. He needed to replenish His soul with time in prayer so off He went up a mountain. When He was ready to rejoin His disciples, He found that the boat had nearly reached the other side of the wind-swept lake. So...Jesus took a shortcut.

The disciples were terrified when they saw Jesus walking on the water toward them, but ever-eager Peter jumped out of the boat to meet Him. Peter walked toward Jesus until he saw the wind. Notice that wording? Peter *saw* the wind. What could that mean?

I think it meant he was distracted by the circumstances surrounding him. Very legitimate, very realistic circumstances. Imagine the thoughts running through his mind: *I'm a fisherman! I know better than this! Walking on water is impossible! What am I doing?! What was I thinking?!*

129

Logic reigned, and Peter sank. He took his focus off Jesus, off the miracle he was experiencing right *at that very moment*, and regretted that he had left the safety of the boat. Jesus, disappointed but merciful, reached out a hand, lifted him up and asked, "Why did you doubt?"

Like Peter, I've been in situations when logic reigned, and I sank. I used to love hanging out in bookstores. The bigger, the better. Until, that is, I decided to write a book. After receiving a mixed response of publisher interest and rejection from proposals for my first novel, I was still in the "waiting mode." While browsing the shelves of a "big box" bookstore, I had a severe meltdown: *What was I thinking? How could I possibly dream of having a book published? Even if, by some remote possibility, my book ever did get published, it would probably end up on the $1 giveaway table.*

I wish I could say that meltdown was a one-time event. It reoccurs every *single* time I go in that bookstore. There are so many better books than mine; so many better writers than me. After visiting the bookstore, I have trouble writing for a day or so; inspiration has evaporated. Aspiring to be a published author makes no sense. Just like Peter's circumstances, the cards are stacked against me. I see the wind, and I start to sink.

Characteristically, Jesus wasn't concerned about circumstances. He was only concerned about Peter's faith and the faith of those in the boat. It's the same for us. The end result God is seeking for us may have nothing to do with publishing success. Far more importantly, He is asking us to stretch our faith, take new risks, and to trust Him. The only requirement is to keep our eyes fixed on Him.

So, today, are you willing to step out of the safety of the boat?

I am. Today, I'm going back to that bookstore.

Prayer: *Merciful Lord, You told the disciples in the boat on that windy night to "Take courage! It is I. Don't be afraid." Give us the courage and confidence to keep writing, to keep submitting our work to editors and publishers, to stay prayerful about our work and its outcome, and to give You our very best. Thank You for the reminder that You are with us and we have nothing to fear. Amen.*

Reflection

What circumstances stop you from writing? Or trying to write?

How do you feel about taking risks with your writing, for example, trying a new genre? Or covering a new topic?

Does anything change when you remind yourself: "The Lord is my helper; I will not be afraid" (Hebrew 13:6)?

A Year of Marketing Flops

"Here's what I've prayerfully come to realize:

This business is a hard one. When a book contract is offered or a store manager buys a book, many things have come into play...and those behind-the-scenes things are mostly out of my control. The things that are somewhat or mostly in my control—the discipline and craft of writing, those marketing efforts I choose to employ, and my relationships—are also going to fluctuate depending on my energy level and what's going on in my life (and in my agent's/editor's/readers' lives). What God requires from me is not success but faithfulness." ~Dena Dyer, author of *The*

Groovy   Chicks'   Road   Trip   to   Love,
www.denadyer.typepad.com

Excerpt from "The Downside of Success"

"The dark side of success can be a marvelous way for us to grow as writers but even more as followers of Jesus Christ. Why do those voices seduce us? What's going on that makes us susceptible to praise? Why do we enjoy and bask in their adulation? What makes them able to seduce us with good things such as appreciation for our talent? What if we saw the problems as coming from our need to be admired, praised, or loved?" ~Cecil Murphey, best-selling author,   speaker,   and   conference   teacher, www.themanbehindthewords.com

"Dear brother and sisters, whenever trouble comes your way, let it be an opportunity for joy. For when your faith is tested, your endurance has a chance to grow. So let it grow, for when your endurance is fully developed, you will be strong in character and ready for anything," (James 1:2-4, NLT). ~Charlotte Holt, author of *Praise the Lord for Roaches!*

"Choose subjects about which you care deeply. This is the best way to remain passionate about your work. Writing can be incredibly draining, and the only way to work through the fatigue is to maintain an inner zeal." ~Craig Alan Hart, Founder of "Christian Fiction On-Line"

"I learned a long time ago that the writing assignments God has given me cannot be written quite as well by anyone else." ~Sally E. Stuart, editor, author of *The Christian Writers' Market Guide*

Not Just Any Arrow

Debora M. Coty

"He has made my mouth like a sharp sword; In the shadow of His hand He has concealed me, and He has also made me a select arrow; He has hidden me in His quiver" (Isaiah 49:2, NAS).

The eve of my 49th birthday waned melancholy as I lay on my back in bed, staring dejectedly at the ceiling. I had just received yet *another* rejection letter from an agent regarding my recently completed book.

It's not that rejection was anything new; I'd collected enough rejection slips during my four years as a professional writer to paper mache a piñata. A big one. Maybe a life-sized rhinoceros. Okay—ten rhinoceroses, six wildebeests, two heifers, and a partridge in a pear tree.

No, rejection per se was not what troubled me. I knew that in the literary game, par for the course is to receive ten rejections to every one acceptance. What bothered me was the nagging suspicion that I'd misheard my calling. That God had said "fight a crook" or "bite a snook" instead of "write a book."

"Lord," I prayed toward the fossilized cobweb in the corner, "Am I hearing you right? I wholeheartedly believed you told me to share the everyday miracles and amazing grace notes you've performed in my life as encouragement for other struggling Christians. But if that's so..." My eyes shifted to the ceiling fan blades above me spinning in perpetual motion but never getting anywhere, much like the carousel of my writing life. "...If that's so, then why is it so blasted hard to find an agent and get this book published? All this effort and I'm getting nowhere. Maybe I should just give up."

Sighing heavily, I reached for my Bible on the nightstand. Propping a pillow behind my back, I randomly flipped worn pages. I felt old. Nearly half a century old. I was writing, but no one was reading. Not my stuff, anyway. What possessed me to think God would actually use *my* words to help anyone? I'm the worst struggler of all in keeping faith through the muck and mire of everyday living.

Glancing down at my opened Bible, my eyes focused on a passage from Isaiah: "He has made my mouth like a sharp sword; in the shadow of His hand He has concealed me, and He has also made me a select arrow; He has hidden me in His quiver."

What was that? My breath stuck in mid-inhale. The anointed words jumped off the page and into my fluttering heart—I knew without a doubt it was a message just for me!

The Lord was telling me that He plans to use my words like a sharp sword, a weapon to cut through Satan's incessantly whispered lies to throw in the towel, to quit trying to push that boulder uphill, to give up the hopeless fight. People need to hear the message of perseverance, and God is quickening my sword by my own experiences in conquering defeat.

My Heavenly Father was sending me a note of encouragement: He will personally take on the enemies before me, running interference with His tall, strong stature so that I can find rest and peace in the protective shadow of His cupped hand. I can't think of a safer place to be.

And best of all, I am a select arrow. Not just any arrow—a *select* arrow. A flint-sharpened, friction-polished, exclusive weapon specially designed to pierce the tough outer shell of God's intended targets and speak God's message to their hearts through the written word. There is no other arrow like me, no person with the exact same background, experiences, and perspective the Lord has given me. I am the only one that can accomplish the task God has *customized* me for.

For now, I am concealed. Undistinguished. Unknown. He has hidden me in His quiver until the right time to use me in battle. Only at that specific time will I be most effective for His glory.

Until then, I will remain content to wait among the other arrows (writers), each to be selected in its own appointed time to fulfill God's designated destiny.

My eyes misted as I read and reread God's personalized message. I felt as if I'd been wrapped in a warm, reassuring blanket of affirmation. I realized the rejections, struggles, disappointments, and failures included in my literary journey were all preparing me to become the select arrow God had in mind all along.

And the exquisite ribbon adorning my 49th birthday gift from my Creator? I was reading the second verse from—where else? Chapter 49, of course.

Prayer: *Lifter of my head, thank You for reminding me that my edict to write is a divine appointment. You alone are the general of my battles, and You've already won the war. Thank You for loving me enough to carve, polish, and sharpen me into a select arrow. When the ordained time comes, make true my course to Your targeted hearts. Amen.*

Reflection

In what way is God planning to use your mouth (words) as a sharp sword?

Name a time when God gave you peace and rest in the protective shadow of His cupped hand. Can you trust that He'll do it again when you need it most?

Stop right now and say these words aloud: God is carving me into a select arrow. Not just *any* arrow. I'm a *select* arrow. Now believe it!

"Write down the thoughts of the moment. Those that come unsought for are commonly the most valuable." ~Francis Bacon, English philosopher (1561-1626)

"I devise a 'Writer's Reading Plan' every January. In that plan, I set a goal of the number of books I intend to read in the coming year (usually between fifty and seventy). Volume is far from my only concern. I pursue a variety of authors, genre, and forms in my reading plan. Such a course of intentional reading does more than broaden my horizons; it broadens me." ~Bob Hostetler, author of *American Idols*, www.bobhostetler.com.

Excerpt from "A Writer's Prayer"

"As I write, guard me from my tendency to laziness, Lord. Nudge me to dig as deep as necessary in researching my story; remind me to use all the tools at my disposal so that I handle the language in a correct, yet creative way. At the same time, don't let me focus so harshly on one 'tree' that I never make it through the 'forest.'" ~Deborah Raney, author of *Remember to Forget* and *A Vow to Cherish*, www.deborahraney.com

Here Are Some Things Publishers are Looking for and Why:

1. Has he or she published any articles in this area? (Why should we invest money in publishing their book, when their writing hasn't been tested anywhere else?)

2. Are they speaking on this topic anywhere? (Marketing money is about as rare as true tithers—if they're not on the road, how can we possibly build a readership?)

3. Do they have any other ideas? (Few "first books" do well—we need to help this person build a career rather than expect to hit the lottery on the first try).

4. Who is their agent? (If they don't have an agent, is that because they couldn't find one? And if they can't find an agent who likes their book, why should we bother to read it?)

5. What kind of platform do they have? (What? They have an email list of 75,000 people who know them? Sold!)

~Gary Thomas, author of *Sacred Marriage*, www.garythomas.com

"It is easy to become anxious or frustrated as we wait to hear from a publisher, but the calming factor is walking in prayer and trusting God for the results." ~Karol Ladd, best-selling author of *The Power of a Positive Woman*, www.positivemom.com

Lessons from the Broom Tree

Joanna Bloss

"This is what the Lord says: 'Stand at the crossroads and look; ask for the ancient paths, ask where the good way is, and walk in it, and you will find rest for your souls." (Jeremiah 6:16, NIV).

I'll never forget the way I felt when I got paid for my first magazine article. Call me shallow, but I think that moment was even more thrilling than seeing my article in print. It was extremely gratifying to know that someone appreciated my work enough to *pay me for it.*

Unfortunately my joy was short-lived. I no sooner got that check in the bank when a rejection letter materialized in my mail box. I completely forgot about all the high I'd experienced only days before. "Whatever." I told myself. "I never wanted to be a writer in the first place."

The one thing that can squelch my writerly enthusiasm quicker than the hot sun melts butter is rejection. It curtails my creativity, destroys my artistry, and throws my inspiration right out the window.

I know writers are supposed to expect rejection. I am fully aware that we're supposed to take it in stride and hit the ground running with the next submission. But I can't help it. Rejection siphons the writer right out of my life.

138

Does rejection ever seem to suck the very life right out of you? If so, maybe you can identify with Elijah. I suppose every job has its downside—even (or maybe especially) if you're a prophet.

In 1 Kings 18 Elijah experiences an amazing victory. God miraculously reveals himself before the 450 prophets of Baal then He empowers Elijah to defeat every last one of them. After that the Lord gives him more power—this time to outrun his mortal enemy Ahab "all the way to Jezreel." Elijah must have been on an enormous high after these intense experiences. Can you just imagine him catching his breath and pausing to compose a praise song? Or maybe gathering up fifty or a hundred of his closest friends and throwing God a big party? Elijah does neither. In fact, when the story picks up in 1 Kings 19, Elijah is still running for his life. By verse three he's had enough. He is beyond tired. He's exhausted, worn out, pushed to the limit. He has nothing left to offer. He is so wiped out that he parks himself under a broom tree and prays for God to take his life. "Right now, Lord—I'm outta here."

One gets the sense that Elijah's exhaustion was far more than physical in nature. Elijah doesn't care that he's been called to be a prophet and doesn't care that the Lord has work for him to do. So he does what I do when I feel overwhelmed. He sleeps and eats—and sleeps some more.

When he regains just enough strength to travel to his next destination, he gets the opportunity to pour out his heart to God. "What's up?" he cries. "I have been working day and night busting my tail for you and all anyone wants to do is kill me. I've had it! I quit!" (1 Kings 19:10, my paraphrase). God patiently listens. And listens some more. I can just imagine Him saying, "Elijah, whenever you're finished with your tantrum, I have some things I want you to hear."

Then God speaks. Not in a loud, crashing, mighty way, but in a gentle whisper. Sweet relief. And God doesn't give Elijah the go ahead to retire and spend his final days resting by the pool in a retirement village in Florida. In fact, He tells him to get right back on the battle field. (Can you hear Elijah groan?) But He does something else as well. He sends in some reinforcement—He gives him Elisha. The battle isn't over, but God is faithful, and Elijah doesn't have to go it alone.

There are some great life lessons in this story. In his exhaustion Elijah does several things that are worth imitating. He allows God to minister to him—he rests and he eats. He cries out to God, and he listens. Finally, he obeys. He gets right back on that horse (figuratively speaking) and gets back on the battlefield.

And this is what I must do—what you must do—when we are faced with rejection and exhaustion, no matter how much we want to give up. Rest, allow God to minister to you, pour your heart out to Him, listen to Him...and write another story. Compose another poem. Schedule another interview or query a different publisher. The important thing is to get right back on the horse and obey the One who empowers you to do more than you could ask or imagine.

Prayer: *Father, I have to admit that I don't handle rejection very well. I hate it when someone tells me they aren't interested in my work. When I am discouraged and worn out, refresh me. Teach me to rest, to allow You to minister to me, and to listen to You. Most importantly help me to keep going and obey You in all that I do. Amen.*

Reflection

In what ways might you be able to relate to Elijah?

What do you need to do most right now...rest? Eat well? Listen to God? Whatever it is, consciously allow Him to minister to you.

Once you're refreshed, what is one way you can proactively get back on that horse?

Ten Ways to Restore Creativity After Experiencing Rejection

1. Tell God how you really feel.
2. Take a walk.
3. Listen to praise music.
4. Prepare and enjoy a delicious meal.
5. Mow the lawn.
6. Write something just for fun.
7. Play with a child.
8. Take a nap.
9. Drink a cup of coffee with a friend.
10. Read something that is fabulously well-written.

~ Joanna Bloss, author of *God's Gifts for the Grad*

"The most valuable lesson I've learned about the writer's life is that it is full of ups and downs. In your own eyes, you will never, ever 'arrive.' Some months you'll be on top and feel wonderful about how things are going; other months you'll be sure your career is over. The sooner you accept that this is normal—and just show up at your desk anyway, day after day after day—the more likely you are to start having more ups than downs. Besides, it's not about you anyway. Though the act of writing may be therapeutic for the writer, a book doesn't really come to life until it's read by someone else. If God uses your story to bring joy or comfort or reproof or wisdom to even one other life, you are a success in the eyes of the only One who matters." ~Deborah Raney, author of *The Clayburn Novels*, www.deborahraney.com

"Use plenty of anecdotes, real life, practical stories, particularly about yourself if appropriate. Sarah, my wife, and I feel strongly that one of the great strengths of Love and Respect is our transparency about our mistakes, how we learned about Love and Respect by trial and error." ~Dr. Emerson Eggerichs, Ph.D., author of *Cracking the Communication Code: The Secret to Speaking Your Mate's Language*, www.loveandrespect.com

Excerpt from "Pushing Through the Pain of Publishing"

"Once you've pressed through the pain of writing your manuscript, another wave of pain threatens to overwhelm you—the pain of finding a publisher who believes in your book like you do. You can feel like a tiny grain of sand on an entire continent of beach, lost in the plethora of other books and authors clamoring for attention. But remember, God sees *every* grain of sand, and He often plucks people out of obscurity especially when your message meets a 'felt need' in His world." ~ Shannon Etheridge, author of the *Every Woman's Battle* series and the *Loving Jesus Without Limits* series, www.shannonetheridge.com

"Let us praise God at all times for His goodness and His faithfulness to inspire beauty—whether it comes through us or someone else." ~Donna Shepherd, author of *Topsy Turvy Land,* www.donnajshepherd.com

Connecting with Readers
Faith Tibbetts McDonald

"Be imitators of God..." (Ephesians 5:1, NIV).

In 1974, just before my sister and I left our shared bedroom in our home in Kenora, Ontario to move 1300 miles to Beaver Falls, Pennsylvania, we wrote a note to the future occupants of the small bedroom—to welcome them and to describe our eight years of living in that space.

In the note we described how we'd talked late into the night, read with flashlights under the covers, and played homemade games that perhaps the future occupants would want to try. Our favorite? Designing sheet and blanket shapes and tucking ourselves into a shape's corner to see if we'd dream about the shape.

On hot summer nights (that far north, I think there were two in the eight years we lived there) we found it most comfortable to sleep—not in the beds—but pressed to the cool tile floor.

In that place, we endured some illnesses. One time, covered with measles and confined to the dimly lit room for three days, I memorized the entire *Alice in Wonderland* sound track by playing it again and again on a record player. Despite the occasional sickness, we said that we'd enjoyed a good life in that room, and we hoped the subsequent occupants did, too.

We wrote the note in our best cursive, folded it carefully, and tucked it inside the closet between the molding and the wall.

A few years later we learned that the children who had moved into the room had found the note and were tickled to read it.

That incident is one of my memory treasures. To write and connect with readers thrills me. That thrill starts in God's heart and makes writers like us tick—especially when we discover how He communicates and that we can imitate Him in action.

God pours ingenuity into communicating. To grasp attention, He doesn't spare a gimmick. He ignited a burning bush that riveted Moses. He painted a rainbow in the sky to seal a deal with Noah. We can ask God for creative ideas to communicate ingeniously with our readers.

God pours substantial time into communication. In His rainbow-sealed words to Noah, He declares that He will remember His promise with people whenever He sees a rainbow. I've searched the Internet and can't find numbers for how many rainbows appear each day, but in all likelihood a rainbow appears somewhere on earth 24/7; therefore, it seems reasonable to conclude that God spends *all* time remembering the promise He made. We can't spend all time contemplating our message, (there are dishes to do) but we imitate God when we invest substantial amounts of time into writing projects.

God does not hoard His words. Ever. He let Balaam's donkey speak them (Numbers 22). God's representative Paul said that it didn't matter why people preached (from false or true motives) as long as the news of Christ was broadcast in every way (Philippians 1:15-18). We are called to write with the same generous spirit.

When we exercise creativity, sacrifice, and generosity in our writing, we are imitating God who designed the thrill of communicating with readers.

Prayer: *Thank you for the thrill of communicating with readers. Please ignite my creativity. Help me invest my resources wisely and enable me to do it all with a giving heart. I long to imitate You. Amen.*

Reflection

What creative risk is God nudging you to take today?

What sacrifice of time or money can you make today to promote the message God has given you to declare?

List one way you can be generous with your writing or speaking talent this week.

"The most valuable lesson I've learned about writing is that it's hard work. Writing is both energizing and draining, something I love to do and sometimes hate to do. Sometimes it's a joy. Sometimes it's like the tenth hour of chopping wood: you just want to be done. It's never done, but eventually it has to be turned in." ~Randy Alcorn, founder, "Eternal Perspective Ministries," author of *Heaven,* www.epm.org

Accepting Criticism

"When you pitch your project to editors and agents at

writers' conferences, listen carefully to their feedback and modify your project accordingly. Editors and agents are in tune with the pulse of the publishing industry. Their advice is meant to help you improve—and succeed." ~Laura Christianson, author of *The Adoption Decision*, www.laurachristianson.com

"When you're facing discouragement, learn how to encourage yourself just as David did (1 Samuel 30:6). Keep a file of "good news" you can read, remind yourself of past accomplishments or make a list of Bible verses that can give you a boost when needed. Find whatever works for you." ~Debra L. Butterfield, author of *Help! My Husband Has Sexually Abused Our Daughter*, www.debralbutterfield.com

"Developing confidence as a writer is no easy task. It can be a painstaking long road filled with lots of bumps and bruises, but the more you remain open-minded, the more your writing craft improves. Developing confidence isn't just about how well you write or how many paid assignments you receive, either. Developing confidence is about learning to be humble—humble enough to take advice and constructive criticism; even when you don't want to." ~Alyce Edrich, author, editor, *The Dabbling Mum*® website, www.thedabblingmum.com

"Write only when the Holy Spirit gives you something to say." ~Janet Kobobel Grant, Literary Agent and founder, Books & Such, Inc.

Running on Empty

Suzanne Woods Fisher

"Your word is a lamp for my feet and a light for my path" *(Psalm 119:105, NIV).*

There are times when writing feels as natural and effortless as breathing. During those times, I lie awake in the still of the morning as an idea comes to life in my mind just waiting to be made visible as a written word. Beginning, middle, conclusion; it all comes together, and I can't wait to get to the computer to spill it out. It will still need work, lots of rewrites, but I've gotten the bones of the piece down.

While writing my first novel, I remember playing a tennis match with actual dialogue of my characters bouncing around in my head. I don't remember how that match turned out, but I do remember the feeling of how *real* my characters seemed and how the conversation they were having (in my head) needed to be written down before it was lost.

After a period of great productivity, suddenly, I'll be emptied of words, like a tipped over water jug. Trying to write a good sentence is akin to constructing an algebraic problem. Not a good thing for me. Words feel stilted, stiff and wooden, and my writing reflects it.

Like most of life, there is a rhythm to writing. Fatigue, stress, busyness, even hormones, can affect that rhythm. Although I do believe that writing is a discipline and that you learn to write by writing, inspiration is evanescent; it isn't something that can be planned for and programmed. And then there's that dreaded writer's block, which originates I think, from anxiety about *getting* writer's block.

When my writing feels like a stream running dry, I've learned to stop fighting it. Instead, I recognize it as a signal. It's an indication that my brain fuel is running low and needs to be refilled. I've even begun to see it as a benefit, the way winter snow improves the land, adding minerals and moisture to weary soil. It can even be a gift from the Lord.

David, who herded sheep as a boy and might have always considered himself primarily a shepherd even as King of Israel, wrote the twenty-third Psalm about God as *his* shepherd. "He maketh me to lie down in green pastures, He leadeth me beside still waters, He restoreth my soul."

A place of plenty and peace, a time to restore basic needs.

God was guiding David's time of rest and replenishment. How many times had David done the same with his own flock, leading them to food and water in perfect security? Sheep need still water because they're easily frightened by rushing water. Just like writers, their anxieties loom large.

Stuck in a stretch when writing words feels like pouring molasses in January, I won't even try to write. Or rather, I don't expect much from my writing. Instead, I read. Good books with phrases that make me hunt for a pen to start underlining.

Making time with the Lord needs to be reprioritized as the first focus of the day. Going to bed a little earlier helps my mind to be renewed. Nurturing tasks like planting bulbs or tilling garden soil reinvigorate me. So do long walks with my goofy Labrador retrievers. I slow down, noticing the way the changing seasons affect my neighborhood.

I try to reflect on what might be causing the word river to dam up in my mind, to see if I can make some self-corrections. Is self-doubt starting to erode my ability to write? Often—too often—it is, and I need to find my way back to relinquish my writing to God for His glory.

By not resisting the dry stretch but instead welcoming it as a time beside still waters and green pastures, I have found that soon the dam will break and the river will run free. I can almost guarantee the same will be true for you.

Prayer: *Lord, You are my shepherd. Please lead me today into places and experiences where my soul will be revived and my passion will be restored. Amen.*

Reflection

Have you ever endured a time in life when you have needed to watch and wait for new green growth? How did it affect your writing?

What is one thing you can do today to re-energize your writing batteries?

Drawing from a Dry Well

"You can't draw from the well of creativity if it's dry. Make time to do whatever fills your well—be it reading, dancing, strolling a garden or art museum, taking in a movie—and resist the urge to consider this time a waste. The non-creative types in our lives often make us feel guilty, be it intentionally or not, for needing alone time to read, think, doodle, zone in front of a movie or with our stereo going, but if we don't refresh our artistic selves, we can't be artistic! Schedule it in, set the money aside, and don't accept excuses from yourself or anyone else—your craft depends on it." ~Alison Strobel, author of *Worlds Collide*, www.alisonstrobel.com

The Writer's Prayer

Open my mind, Lord.
Grant me the talent to write with clarity and style
So my words go down rich and smooth like fine wine
And leave my reader thirsty for more.

Open my heart, Lord.
Grant me the sensitivity to understand my characters
—their hopes, their wants, their dreams—
And help me to confer that empathy to my reader.

Open my soul, Lord,
So I may be a channel to wisdom and creativity
From beyond my Self.
Stoke my imagination with vivid imagery and vibrant perception.

But most of all, Lord,
Help me to know the Truth,
So my fiction is more honest than actuality
And reaches the depths of my reader's soul.

Wrap these gifts with opportunity, perseverance,
And the strength to resist those who insist it can't be done. Amen.
~© 1999 Sandy Tritt, author of *Everything I Know*, editor, www.InspirationForWriters.com

"Becoming a publishable writer is a multi-year project. When a publisher buys your book, they are risking tens of thousands of dollars that you will at least break even. Would you risk that much money on someone who'd only been writing a few weeks? Neither will an editor." ~Randy Ingermanson, publisher, Advanced Fiction Writing E-zine, Christy award-winning author of *Transgression* and *Oxygen*, www.ingermanson.com

"For book proposals: Find some great examples from CBA websites and ask for some from published writers. Then take the best of these, modeling their format, and build your own winning book proposal." ~Trish Berg, author of *Rattled* and *The Great American Supper Swap*, www.trishberg.com

"Have faith, do your homework, and get a system. Editors and agents are just as insecure as you are about what constitutes 'good' writing. *Estate Sale* was rejected 18 times before it found the right home." ~Stacy Gillett Coyle, award-winning poet, *Cloud Seeding*

Thou Shalt Not Criticize Me

Debora M. Coty

"So humble yourselves under the mighty power of God, and in His good time He will honor you" (1 Peter 5:6, NLT).

"Please consider changing the age of the protagonist," my editor's voice entreated over the phone. "I feel strongly about this. I truly think it will enhance the storyline and make the book marketable to a wider audience."

"Well, I'll think about it," I said, shaking my head. *In a June blizzard, maybe*, I thought. *It's my story. I'm no rookie; I know what's best.*

After my manuscript's sixth rejection, I began to rethink my previous self-righteous attitude. Why did I feel so defensive about her suggestions? Isn't that why I hired an editor in the first place—to give me helpful criticism? My humility was complete when I received an agent's blunt personal note: "Why did you make the main character so young? There is no market for this book. Not ever."

As writers, we receive more than our fair share of criticism about our work. From editors, agents, publishers, even readers. Sometimes, the most helpful suggestion grates on our nerves.

The bottom line is that we consider our work a precious, sacred creation like, well, a baby. What we really want is someone to admire our beautiful new baby. Instead, they tell us to transfer his ear to his kneecap, turn his head around backwards, remove his feet, and add an appendage.

So how do we conquer that menacing defensive reaction that suddenly blazes up from our innards when we face these well-meaning critics?

We must remind ourselves that criticism from knowledgeable sources provides potential for growth. "If you listen to constructive criticism, you will be at home among the wise. If you reject criticism, you only harm yourself; but if you listen to correction, you grow in understanding" (Proverbs 15:31-32).

Granted, in some cases, criticism may be elicited by jealousy, bad faith, or just plain malicious intent to do us harm. Consider the source and pray for discernment.

Criticism helps reveal our true selves by exposing our blind spots. "Get all the advice and instruction you can, and be wise the rest of your life." (Proverbs 19:20). There are some things about ourselves we simply can't see. When others point out these hidden flaws, we must ask ourselves, "Could this be true, even in part?"

I generally write like I speak. This choice of style is not necessarily a bad thing, but when you're a hick from the sticks like me, ya gotta be plum keerful who 'tis yer speakin' at. An English teacher once gently suggested that I "sophisticate" my vocabulary a bit. I took offense, grousing that God made me who I am—warts and all—and uppity folks who don't cotton to my vernacular *shorely* don't have to read it.

The result, of course, was that they didn't.

In the blind throes of defensiveness, I neglected to consider that God also supplies wart remover for those desiring to improve themselves. After a few classes in grammatical sentence structure—and lots of effort—at least I sounded like an *educated* bumpkin. (You can take the girl out of the country, but you're nigh on stupefied if you reckon on taking the country out of the girl!)

If we are open to constructive criticism, we can often avoid mistakes, detouring failure and subsequent pain. And those detours are the kind we should happily go out of our way to follow.

Here in Florida we get lots of sinkholes—earth-swallowing pits that open up unexpectedly, occasionally devouring roads, trees, and even houses. My neighbor stepped out of his car onto the grass beside his driveway and felt his shoe get sucked off his foot. He hopped back onto the pavement and watched his loafer disappear into a thirty-foot chasm.

Occasionally you'll see a picture in the newspaper of a car nose down in a sinkhole because the owner failed to heed detour signs.

Accepting and learning from critique offered in good faith is like taking a detour to avoid career sinkholes. Would we intentionally drive the car we paid hard-earned money for into a gaping orifice? So why would we carelessly ignore warning signs that may save the literary career we've poured our hearts into from ruin?

As we grow in wisdom and words, God promises to use those skills to honor us as we honor Him. "If you ignore criticism, you will end in poverty and disgrace; if you accept criticism, you will be honored" (Proverbs 13:18).

Best of all, criticism increases our potential for success. We learn to follow in the footsteps of the writers who impacted our lives, thereby helping others on their own life paths. "People who accept correction are on the pathway to life, but those who ignore it will lead others astray" (Proverbs 10:17).

As a happy ending to the opening anecdote, I eventually came to my senses, heeded the wise editor's advice, and rewrote the protagonist's age. Four months later, I signed a publishing contract for *The Distant Shore.*

Nobody likes to hear they're in need of change. But if we're not told, how will we know? A "my way or the highway" attitude permeating a writing ministry only serves to strangle growth and dishonor the One in whose name we toil.

We can respond to criticism by becoming better...or bitter. Which will *you* choose?

Prayer: *Father, make me humble. Help me to accept constructive criticism as the loving rod of correction from Your mighty hand; a Biblical and necessary means to the end of glorifying You through the very best of my literary potential. Amen.*

Reflection

Name two times when you had difficulty accepting critique of your work. Why was the criticism so hard to swallow?

Can you think of a blind spot in your work that was uncovered by helpful criticism?

List three practical approaches to accepting criticism that can help you become better at your writing craft, not bitter.

"*He guides the humble in what is right and teaches them his way*" (Psalm 25:9).

5 Things a Rejection Letter Can Never Take Away from Me

1) *My accomplishment.* I wrote, revised, and completed an article, poem, or book that expressed my heart. Many writers have that same intention but not the ability to follow through and finish.

2) *My self-esteem.* A standardized form letter informing me that my work isn't good enough is not worth taking seriously as an assessment of my talent. (And most rejection letters are "canned" responses to effectively end conversation about that particular project.)

3) *My calling.* Writing has been given to me as a call from the Lord.

4) *My clear vision.* I won't allow that letter to minimize my successes and magnify my failures.

5) *My hope.* And the determination to try again.

~Suzanne Woods Fisher, author of *Copper Star* and *Copper Fire*

Excerpt from "Writer's Prayers"

"Father, shield me from impatience.
I choose to seek your time and plan.
Let me not run ahead nor lag behind,
as I wait for your wish and command."

~ Sally Jadlow, author of *The Late Sooner*, www.sallyjadlow.com

"Stay determined, even after you get published. Preston Sturges, the legendary writer-director, once said, 'When the last dime is gone, I'll sit on the cub with a pencil and a ten-cent notebook and start the whole thing all over again.' Try

to keep that attitude, no matter where your writing goes."
~James Scott Bell, best-selling novelist, former fiction
columnist for *Writer's Digest* and author of *Write Great
Fiction: Plot and Structure,* www.jamesscottbell.com

"Faith and fear cannot reside together. Either I fear the future or have faith in Jesus. I choose faith!" ~Tricia Goyer, author of *Life Interrupted*, www.triciagoyer.com

Fearing Failure

Suzanne Woods Fisher

"For I am the Lord, your God, who takes hold of your right hand and says to you, Do not fear; I will help you" (Isaiah 41:13, NIV).

Emily Dickinson wrote nearly two thousand poems. Less than ten were published in her lifetime, anonymously—most likely without her knowledge. Obsessively reclusive, she kept them hidden in her room, unseen, discovered by her family after her death. She died never knowing how the public would respond to her talent. She had no idea that she would be considered one of America's quintessential poets.

What kept Emily from sharing her life work with others? Even her sister had no idea of the volume of material she wrote. What stopped her?

Sometimes I wonder how much of it might have been an acute fear of failure.

Fear of failure has been my biggest obstacle as a writer. When I was just starting out as a freelancer, I actually turned down writing assignments and speaking opportunities because of a crippling fear that I would fail. It was hard enough to send out material, the best-of-my-ability kind of work, on speculation. And then to wait. Hoping, praying, it would be accepted. More often than not, it wasn't.

Rejection was—is—the norm. So is discouragement. It doesn't take much to dispirit a new writer.

A year ago, an editor returned a manuscript to me with the comment that the writing wasn't up to her publishing house's "caliber." *Ouch!* That was a tough remark to swallow. But I did. I gulped down my pride and asked her for editorial comments which she gave me. I read them carefully, incorporated what I could, and then I moved on.

I didn't wallow. I didn't stop writing. I didn't feel wounded. In fact, truthfully, I didn't agree with her assessment. Instead, I kept improving the manuscript, sent it out to other publishers, and eventually, received a book contract. I've developed a very thick skin, taking rejection in stride so it doesn't derail me as it has in the past.

So what changed for me?

It started when my daughter ran for class treasurer of her high school freshman class. The night of the election, she received news that she had lost. I found her sobbing on her bed and sat down next to her, not saying anything for a while. After her sobs drizzled to sniffles, I told her that I was proud of her for trying. *Just for trying.* For being willing to take a risk. She did something that ninety-nine percent of the student body couldn't do. I couldn't have been prouder of her if she had won or not; I only cared that she was willing to *try.*

Suddenly, it dawned on me that God was rooting for me, with my writing, in the same way I was rooting for my daughter. He wasn't *waiting* to be proud of me until I was successful. He already *was* proud. By continuing to write, I was willing to face my fear of failure, trust Him, and just keep trying.

Scripture confirmed my revelation: "I'm confident of this, that God who began a good work in you will carry it onto completion until the day Jesus returns" (Phil 1:6). And "Let us therefore come boldly unto the throne of grace, that we may obtain mercy, and find grace to help in time of need" (Hebrews 4:16, KJV).

Over and over, I bumped into those two words: confidence and boldness. I started to believe, to truly believe, that the best fix for my fear was grasping God's personal, unshakable commitment to my well-being.

Little by little, failure became less of a big fear. I've concluded if the worst thing I face in life is a ton of rejection letters, well, I can handle that. My confidence rests in God alone.

By the way, my daughter ran for class treasurer in her sophomore year, too. And lost. Then she ran again in her junior year and garnered the most votes. But I think she really won in the first election—maybe not with votes, but with something far more important.

Prayer: *Keeper of my heart, deliver me from my fears and teach me to relinquish them to You. And thank You for never giving up on me. Amen.*

Reflection

What is your biggest obstacle to completing a writing project?

What wears you out as a writer? What discourages you the most?

How can you allow the Lord to set you free from those obstacles?

When you remind yourself: "The Lord is my helper; I will not be afraid" (Hebrew 13:6), does anything change for you?

"You may be disappointed if you fail, but you are doomed if you don't try." ~Beverly Sills, American opera singer (born 1929)

"Learn the craft of writing so you can effectively share God's story." ~Susan Kelly Skitt, speaker, author of *The One Year Life Verse Devotional*, www.livingtheadventurouslife.blogspot.com

"We all pray for the flowing rivers, but sometimes all the streams in the desert have dried up. I recommend Psalm 42. All our writing has to flow from the source. You can't have characters that are growing spiritually if you aren't growing spiritually." ~Donna Fletcher Crow, author of *The Cambridge Chronicles series*

"Writing is not for the faint of heart. It takes a lot of hard work, determination, patience, perseverance, and faith. And it won't happen overnight. You have to maintain a teachable spirit and be open to constructive criticism, no matter how far along in your writing journey you get. In the end, the rewards far outweigh all the sweat and tears you shed along the way. Most importantly, if you feel this is the path for you, never give up!" ~Amber Miller, author of *Promises, Promises,* www.ambermiller.com

I Don't Have the Faintest Inkling...

The work *inkling* means a vague idea. It can be traced back to days when writing was done with a pen made of a wooden handle with a steel nib attached to it. The writer dipped his nib into a bottle of ink or an inkwell and then wrote until the ink on the nib ran out, usually after a few words. Then he dipped again. One advantage was that the writer had to pause every few seconds to dip his pen in the bottle of ink and this gave him time to reflect and think about what he was writing. Hence, the phrase, "I don't have the faintest inkling..."

"Never allow the rat race or relentless pace to take the color and energy out of yours days. Who cares if we can construct a perfect sentence if there is no life or substance behind our words?" ~Susie Larson, freelance writer, speaker, author of *Balance that Works When Life Doesn't*, www.susielarson.com

Revisions
Faith Tibbetts McDonald

"And the words of the Lord are flawless, like silver refined in a furnace of clay, purified seven times" (Psalm12:6, NIV).

According to the first chapter of the book of Genesis, after God created earth and mankind He reflected and concluded that everything He had made was good.

Just a few chapters later, man's behavior compelled God to re-evaluate the state of His masterpiece. "The Lord was grieved that He had made man on the earth, and his heart was filled with pain. So the Lord said, "I will wipe mankind, whom I have created, from the face of the earth" (Genesis 6:6-7).

How's that for revision of mammoth proportions?

My own writing revisions have always been on a smaller scale, but the feelings associated with creating and later revamping my work seem similar to those attributed to God in Genesis. When I consider a finished manuscript, I think: *Good. Very good.* After an interval, when I'm compelled to re-examine my words, perhaps at an editor's request, I think: *This needs work.*

I grieve as I subsequently reshape my piece and consider deleting phrases and paragraphs that I had once so carefully crafted. It's painful to throw my work away. I've found that four perspectives help me revise with resolve. First, I acknowledge that the feelings of grief. God felt pain in revamping and so do I. I know that revising is going to hurt. The pain is genuine, but I press on knowing that the end result will be a better piece. In his classic book *On Writing Well* William Zinsser encourages writers to be thankful for every word, phrase, and sentence they can delete from their work. Concise writing is clear writing. I try to follow his advice and go beyond grief to practice gratitude in the pruning process.

Second, I remember that although my piece seems *good, very good* there is always room in my work for improvement. Are there phrases or sentences that must be clarified? Are there concrete, specific details to include that will communicate the message more vividly? Are there vague verbs that must be replaced with vigorous verbs?

Third, I determine to submit graciously to my reader or editor. If the reader says the words don't communicate, I resist the urge to stridently claim, *If you were more intelligent you'd understand*...A request for revision is a good time to practice Ephesians' teaching, "Submit to one another out of reverence for Christ" (Ephesians 5:21).

Fourth, I ask God to enable me to see the good in the piece, the reason I wrote it in the first place. Sometimes, in the frenzy of revision, I get to the point of longing to eradicate every word, wipe out every punctuation mark, and start from scratch. It was especially fun—two decades ago—when I wrote with a typewriter, to rip the printed page from the typewriter, give the carriage a twirl, crumple the paper, and toss it in a corner. As convenient as computers make writing, they miss the mark when it comes to ultimate revision. Pressing a computer delete key lacks the drama of ripping and crumpling.

When God determined to complete His ultimate revision, He saw and saved Noah, a righteous man who found favor in God's eyes (Genesis 6:8). Similarly, revising writers must scour their work for redeeming thoughts and eloquent sentences. Let them stand the test of revision.

Just as our revisions will never approach God's in significance, our words will never be flawless like His. However, our goal is to offer Him words that have been refined by revision, like silver refined in a furnace of clay, into the best we can craft.

Prayer: *Lord, help me overcome the disappointment I feel when I must revamp or throw away some of my creation. Help me humbly listen to suggestions to improve my work I want to offer You the best possible manuscript that I am capable of creating. Amen.*

Reflection

Write down some of the feelings you have when an editor or reader mentions that your piece requires revision. Don't deny them or bottle them up. Telling the truth about feelings is the first step to channeling them into action.

Create a computer file where you can keep the sentences (or paragraphs) you delete from a piece. It's very likely that you will be able to use them in another piece someday.

"When people ask me, 'How do you get published?' My first question to them is, 'How badly do you want it?' I feel that getting that first book published takes as much time, energy, and money as it takes to pursue a Master's Degree." ~Ellie Kay, America's Family Financial Expert®, best-selling author of eleven books, www.elliekay.com

"Do your research. Book publishing is a business just like any other. Read up on all the ins and outs of query letters, book proposals, and writing techniques, so you can present your manuscript in the best possible light." ~Linda Danis, best-selling author of *365 Things Every New Mom Should Know*

"Before I begin the first sentence of the first chapter, I write a personality profile and physical description of each major character. If a house, office building, or other structure is important to the action, I draw a floor plan and briefly describe the décor. I do a timeline that begins with the plot situation and work backwards. This takes a lot of self-discipline, because all the time I'm doing this preparation work I'm just bursting to get started telling the story. However, the up-front work pays off. If I want to drop an event into a character's past, the timeline allows me to set the date easily because the math has already been done." ~Stephanie Redmont, author of *Lord I'm Coming Home*, www.sredmont.com

"Take the first step in faith; you don't have to see the whole staircase, just take the first step." ~submitted by Michelle Dragalin, fiction and non-fiction writer

"It's easy for me to become so focused on getting my words in print that I ignore the needs of others around me. God has shown me it's important to be published in lives. If I'm so busy writing I can't take time for my family and friends then my priorities are wrong." ~Lydia E. Harris, contributor to *Blessed Among Women: God's Gifts to Mothers,* www.lydiaeharris.com

When God Closes a Door

Joanna Bloss

"Now listen, you who say, 'Today or tomorrow we will go to this or that city, spend a year there, carry on business and make money.' Why, you do not even know what will happen tomorrow...Instead, you ought to say, 'If it is the Lord's will, we will live and do this or that'" (James 4:13, 15 NIV).

What are your goals as a writer?

Maybe your agenda looks something like this: break into magazines by writing special interest pieces for my local newspaper. Get magazine articles published and begin a monthly column. After writing a successful monthly column (and building a killer platform) for a couple years (all the while working on the next great American novel), I'll pitch my brilliant book to the thousands of publishers who are pounding down my door. I'll negotiate a lucrative contract, cash my million dollar advance, and enjoy all the free publicity that surrounds the release of my bestseller. After years of writing profitable tomes, I'll retire from my regular writing and pen my memoirs from my seaside villa...

Okay, so I'm exaggerating. But you do have an agenda, right? How does your writing agenda stack up against God's plan for your life?

When I think of a guy who really understands God's agenda, I think of Paul. Paul's whole post-conversion life is completely devoted to doing what God wants him to do. That's why it kind of surprises me to read verses like Acts 16:6-7. Verse 6 says that Paul and his companions were "kept by the Holy Spirit from preaching the word in the province of Asia" and verse 7 says "they tried to enter Bithynia, but the Spirit of Jesus would not allow them to." The text doesn't skip a beat when it says (in a nutshell) that when the door slammed shut, Paul and friends seamlessly move on to the window. Plan B.

In my life, when God closes a door that I clearly thought He opened, I do not move on to the window quite so graciously. It's more like, "What? I thought you told me to do X. Now that's not working out! What's up with that? Why did you change the plan without consulting me?"

Sometimes I don't doubt God, I doubt myself. "Maybe I wasn't listening closely enough. Maybe I was just going out and doing my own thing and God had to stop me before I spun out of control." "Maybe He wants me to quit entirely." "Maybe I completely misinterpreted my call."

You get the picture. When circumstances don't cooperate with my best laid plans, I tend to get a little panicky. This is the problem with best-laid plans.

We've all fallen into the trap of making plans then praying en route as we accomplish them. I'm pretty sure that's not how God wants us to operate. But how do we tell the difference between doing our own thing and obediently following God's leading? How did Paul know that when the door closed to Asia they should go to Galatia?

Sometimes we have a tendency to depend far too much on circumstances, but on the other hand, how else are we going to know what He wants us to do? I don't know about you, but I certainly haven't had any burning-bush encounters lately.

I think the key is *listening* and then proceeding. Immersing ourselves in God's word. Regularly. Earnestly praying for insight, wisdom, and direction. Asking Him to lead us on the path He wants us to take. When doors close, rather than doubting, we stop and ask Him what to do next. Then *listen* again. We should be so thoroughly saturated with the Holy Spirit that we instinctively know what God is calling us to do.

This must have been what transpired with Paul and his companions. They prayed and listened then obeyed. When a door closed they waited, listened, and went on to the next step.

When rejection comes your way, it doesn't mean you shouldn't have submitted that piece to that publisher, or that you are a bad writer, or that God hasn't called you to write. And, rejection doesn't mean the same thing every time to every writer. The only way to discern the next step is to ask God and then to listen. Check with Him then make your plans, allowing Him to lead you every step of the way.

Prayer: *Heavenly Father, it is so tempting for me to take off and work towards accomplishing my own agenda without giving Yours much thought at all. Forgive me for making plans without consulting You. Forgive me for making decisions without considering what You want for my life. Help me to listen intently to You and to gently follow Your leading. Amen.*

Reflection

When was the last time a door slammed shut for you?

What was your gut reaction?

What do you think God is leading you to do in this situation?

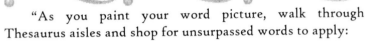

"As you paint your word picture, walk through Thesaurus aisles and shop for unsurpassed words to apply:
1. Velcro® nouns
2. Zealous Verbs
3. A Spattering of Multihued Adjectives
-Arlene Knickerbocker, editor, teacher, author of *Open the Door to Another Realm,* www.thewritespot.org

"Writing is like this weird endless cycle of neediness. It evolves in incremental steps of if onlys:

1. If only I could be published in a magazine, even if I'm not paid.
2. If only I could be paid to be published in a magazine.
3. If only I could go to a writer's conference and have an agent show interest in my proposal.
4. If only I could sign with an agent.
5. If only that agent could sell my work.
6. If only I could have more than one contract.
7. If only I could earn out the advance for the book I wrote.
8. If only I could sell enough books so a publisher would want another book from me
9. If only a publisher would treat a midlist author like me kindly.

10. If only I could make a living at writing.
That's a lot of if onlys!"
~Mary E. DeMuth, author of *Building the Christian Family You Never Had*, www.relevantprose.com

"The Scriptures tell us to be a joy for our pastors. In a similar way, I think we should be a joy for our editors and publishers. By God's grace, be humble and gracious, thus honoring the Lord in the entire process." ~Martha Peace, Biblical counselor and author of *The Excellent Wife*, www.marthapeace.com

"As an editor, I can honestly say that I hate giving rejections just as much as I hate receiving them. But I've learned a few things over the years. Rejections aren't always about you, the person, or your talents as a writer. Sometimes, rejections are simply a matter of already covering certain materials, having a similar article assigned to another writer, or not having enough space or funds to buy more articles." ~Alyce Edrich, author, editor, *The Dabbling Mum*® website, www.thedabblingmum.com

"A Christian writer *must* keep a strong and vibrant relationship with the Lord in order to have something of spiritual significance to say. Otherwise all we're giving is opinion, and our readers have a perfect right to ignore that. Thoughts gleaned from time with the Lord are something else again, and readers ignore them at their own peril." ~Gayle Roper, bestselling author of *A Woman and Her Emotions,* www.gayleroper.com

Stuck In Crete

Debora M. Coty

"The reason I left you in Crete was that you might straighten out what was left unfinished..." (Titus 1:5, NIV).

Like Titus, all of us have been stuck in Crete at one time or another. Some of us are there now.

In New Testament times, the remote island of Crete wasn't such a terrific place to be. Paul lamented that "the people of Crete are all liars; they are cruel animals and lazy gluttons" (Titus 1:12). Yet because of his administrative gifts, Paul left his beloved assistant, Titus, there to sort out the fledgling church's mess and organize the Christian converts. Not likely a mission Titus would volitionally choose, but Paul had faith that Titus would positively influence Crete, rather than Crete negatively influencing Titus.

The Crete we often get stuck in today isn't the geographical island.

No, the Crete I'm referring to is a mindset—a unique, personal space designated to us. A place we'd rather *not* be; a place that may involve isolation, stress, or even misery; a place where our assignment is to stay put until God sends us elsewhere.

In the writing profession, Crete is that seemingly endless wasteland called *waiting*: Literary Limboland, Publication Purgatory, The Manuscript Netherworld. That yawning black hole that devours our creative energies while swallowing great chunks of time into its darkest chasm. It feels like perpetual pregnancy—you're constantly anticipating a baby that is never delivered.

God may choose to leave us in our own Crete for a time as Paul left Titus. He may want us to clean up unfinished business or to accomplish specific tasks before we move on. Or He may be developing within us the patience and trust necessary to wait for His will in His timing.

Titus was a wonderful role model of how to not only exist in Crete but to productively and creatively prosper. According to 2 Corinthians, chapters 7 and 8, despite trying circumstances, he accepted his appointed job and maintained a joyful attitude. Titus didn't pout about his "unfair" situation. He realized that his immediate discomfort was allowed by God to stretch his personal parameters. He knew that he was where he was supposed to be and found joy in submission to God's plan.

Over a fourteen-month period, I was asked to do two rewrites on a national magazine article. I complied (smiling through gritted teeth), only to have the editor inform me that she decided *not* to use the piece. After I'd licked my wounds, God nudged me to capitalize on the relationship I had established with the editor while working on the story. I boldly bypassed the query stage and submitted another manuscript, which she promptly accepted.

During those fourteen months in Crete, publication and paycheck hovered on the horizon just out of reach. Like Titus, I was left in a place I really didn't wish to be. But afterward, I realized that without my extended stay in Crete, I wouldn't have developed a relationship with the editor that resulted in achievement of my goal. There was a larger picture I couldn't see as God stretched my parameters of faith.

2 Corinthians 8 describes other qualities Titus honed in Crete: hard work, earnestness, and taking initiative. He didn't mess around—Titus *looked* for work to be done and then did it to the best of his ability. He proved his trustworthiness in tasks great and small, justifying Paul's faith in the leadership of a Greek (Gentile) convert to Christianity, which at the time was rather rare in the predominantly Jewish early church.

When I'm glaring at my empty mailbox or checking my e-mail inbox for the tenth time that day, I often feel stuck in Crete. Spider webs sprout on my "Accepted for Publication" file. I do a desperate "rain dance," hopping on one foot around my computer. Where is that editor's overdue response? What do you mean a two-year lead time?

Why, oh, why is this business so besotted with waiting, waiting, and more waiting?

I've discovered that the very reason I want to leave Writer's Crete is the reason God left me there. My character needs editing. God, the supreme Editor-in-Chief, is perfecting the manuscript of my life. His eraser chafes, and His pen digs deep. Crafting patience isn't pleasant. It drives me batty. But the final draft is unshakable trust in God's omnipotent timing.

Prayer: *Lord, help me to find joy in submission to Your assignments and to realize that, even in Crete, You are constantly stretching me to new parameters. Amen.*

Reflection

What personal Crete are you currently stuck in? What unfinished business may God want you to take care of there?

List three creative ways you can find joy in submission to God's plan to wait in Crete.

Could *your* character possibly need editing? Name at least two traits that God may be honing and refining during your stay in Crete.

"Bottom line, it takes months sometimes for a manuscript to be seriously processed, championed, and considered. Three months isn't long in book publishing when it comes to this process. I know the writer is sitting around waiting—well don't. Write another proposal. Get another magazine article out there. Don't fixate on the single project. Because if you push, you can get an answer—but not the one you want." ~Terry Whalin, editor, Whalin Literary Agency

Little Known Fact

C.S. Lewis received more than 800 rejection letters before selling his first book. ~source: *Colossal Collection of "Quotable" Quotes*, Bathroom Readers' Press

"As an author, I've always tried to promote my books as much as possible. However, now that I'm on the other side of the fence as a Publicity Director for a publishing house, I understand the importance of author involvement in the campaign. Promoting a book requires teamwork and cooperation between the marketing staff, publicist, and author. If an author is passionate, sincere, and understanding, their publicist will be, too." ~Carla Williams, author, Editorial and Publicity Director, WinePress Publishing Group

"Why be envious of other writers? I must believe God has a message inside this container of clay that only I can write. I ask God to replace jealousy with trust. I do trust in His plan, His will, and His purpose for me." ~Donna Shepherd, author of *Topsy Turvy Land*, www.donnajshepherd.com

"Always have two to three books in progress on the back burner. When you go stale on one, flip to the other and work on that." ~Trish Berg, author of *Rattled* and *The Great American Supper Swap*, www.trishberg.com

Trust and Obey

Faith Tibbetts McDonald

"And I gave them My statutes and showed them My judgments, which, if a man does, he shall live by them." (Ezekiel 20:11, NKJV).

If you're looking for a quick pick-me-up, I don't recommend the book of Ezekiel. It's filled with bad news and heart-wrenching lament.

Even so, it is possible to walk away with some positives insights from Ezekiel—such as a piqued curiosity about intriguing word pictures like "wheels-a-rolling" and "rims with eyes in them," or about the writer mentioned in Chapter 9. He's a man clothed in linen who carries a writing kit or writer's inkhorn and who completes a difficult writing assignment. While I'd hesitate to sign up for a writing task like the one God assigns him, I admire his obedience. I'm inspired to emulate him. Maybe you will be, too.

Here, according to Ezekiel, is the writer's story: "and the Lord said to him, 'Go through the midst of the city, through the midst of Jerusalem, and put a mark on the foreheads of the men who sigh and cry over all the abominations that are done within it'." So the writer obeyed God's request and made his marks.

Then the Lord ordered guards to kill all unmarked people: Obliterate them all. Don't show compassion (from

Ezekiel 9: 5, 7). The unmarked people were violent Israelites who were involved in vile, detestable practices. The marking and the killing takes place in a vision in which God reveals to Ezekiel the dire consequences of His people's evil choices.

Like I mentioned, Ezekiel's *not* a diverting read. But we can learn from that writer. First of all, he's clothed in linen. Linen is a commodity of beauty and utility, and it symbolizes status according to the *Dictionary of Biblical Imagery* by Leland Ryken, James C. Wilhoit, and Tremper Longman III. God clothed the writer in linen because He esteemed the writer. God regarded the writer's task as significant.

So that's lesson number one: Picture God laying out a linen outfit for you to pull on before you sit down at the computer. Extravagantly dressed—looking good and fitted for work, approach your task with mindfulness and reverence. Know that your task teems with God-endowed meaning.

Lesson two is that God tells the writer what to do. Dressed and prepared for work, we must listen to God's instructions. God promises to instruct us, but sometimes His instruction is subtle. Before you set to write, pause and ask God to direct your heart and mind.

That leads to the third lesson: Obey. Even if you don't understand God's command or the rationale behind it, even if the task seems overwhelming—obey.

I admire the writer mentioned in Ezekiel most for his prompt, trusting obedience. If God had told me that my writing task was to mark on people's foreheads, I'd have sputtered doubts and come up with reasons to avoid the task. If God allowed, I'm convinced we'd still be standing there, and I'd be trying to negotiate my way to a writing assignment that made more sense to me.

"But why do you want me to put *a mark* on their foreheads?" (Or, in my own wording, *"But why do you want me to write on **that** topic?"*)

"Are you sure you want me to write it *on foreheads?"* (*Are sure you want me to query **that** magazine?*)

"And what if someone mistakes my work for a tattoo?" *(What if my friends or family don't understand **why** I wrote on that subject?)*

"All right then. What color should the mark be?" *(Should I write my rough draft at the computer, or should I go to Starbucks and write long hand in my journal?)*

"This is way too much responsibility for me. What if I miss someone?" *(What if I don't clearly convey the idea you've given me and confuse a reader?)*

The writer mentioned in Ezekiel didn't waste time or effort negotiating. He promptly and diligently set about completing the assigned task and when he was finished, he reported, "I have done as You commanded me" (Ezekiel 9: 11).

His obedient attitude is one I long to emulate. I want to trust God even when I don't understand the task He sets before me. Perhaps I need to write without a promise of publication. Perhaps I need to write in the face of probable rejection.

Like the writer committed to listen to God, I need to ask God to put His commands in my heart. We can rely on Him to do that. In one of the verses that makes Ezekiel well worth the read, He promises, "I will put My Spirit within you and cause you to walk in My statutes, and you will keep My judgments and do them" (Ezekiel 36:27).

And like the writer committed to complete his God-assigned task, I need to respond wholeheartedly and diligently when God assigns me a writing task.

Prayer: *Thank you for clothing me in linen. I want to listen carefully as You describe the writing task You want me to complete today. I want to complete it carefully and skillfully. Please give me what it takes. I, too, want to report, "I have done as You commanded me." Amen.*

Reflection

List two times when you obeyed God's instructions even when you didn't understand the "why" behind them. List one time you didn't obey.

List three specific steps you can take to get past your tendency to negotiate, make excuses, or procrastinate.

Just What *Is* an Inkhorn?

The inkhorn was an actual horn from an animal used as an inkwell. It was worn by writers in their girdle, like the writer in Ezekiel 9:2-3,11. To modern ears, an inkhorn is a derogatory term for a pedantic or ostentatious writer.

"It's a funny thing: the more I practice, the luckier I get." ~Arnold Palmer, American professional golfer (born 1929)

"Don't be afraid to hire an editor when your first 'big' project is complete. I remember the first time I paid someone to edit my work. It was filled with so many red marks, suggestions, and tips that I literally cried. I couldn't even fathom the idea of going back and 'fixing' all those red marks. All I wanted to do was toss the material in the trash and quit writing. But after a good cry and a call to my copy editor, I sat down and got to work. The result: a project I can honestly say I am very proud of!" ~Alyce Edrich, author, editor, *The Dabbling Mum*® website, www.thedabblingmumb.com

"Be intentional. One of the first questions to ask yourself is: who am I writing this for? If the answer is 'Christians', then pray and search your heart, asking God to give you a message He wants His Church to hear. If the answer is 'those who don't have faith in Christ', then pray God will lead you to the story He wants you to tell for that audience. And then seek the appropriate publisher who will market your book to that particular audience. You'll end up with a much more powerful book by asking these purposeful questions beforehand." ~Lisa Samson, award-winning author of *Justice in the Burbs,* http://lisasamson.typepad.com

"Don't run the risk of giving anyone a reason to turn Jesus down. Your work is an offering to God. Take all the time you need to present it whole and unblemished." ~Athol Dickson, author of *River Rising*, www.atholdickson.com

Cracked Mirrors
Debora M. Coty

"We put no stumbling block in anyone's path, so that our ministry will not be discredited" (2 Corinthians 6:3, NIV).

"You call this finished?" the editor's gravelly voice interrogated.

"Well, yes. I did the rewrite to your specifications." Elise's knuckles whitened on the telephone receiver while her brain rebutted, *At eight cents a word, you get what you pay for, Tightwad!*

"So how long did you spend on it, ten minutes?"

"It took four days, *Sir*, and I put a lot of thought into it. You said you needed it ASAP, so I shoved everything else aside. Now I'm behind on my other deadlines." Elise doubted her barely disguised sarcasm was evident to this insensitive chump.

"Hmmph. Well, I'll give you one more shot, kid. If it still reeks like month-old mullet, I'm turning the assignment over to a more experienced writer."

How would you respond in this situation?

As Christians in a sometimes cutthroat profession, we must be aware of our Godly influence slip-sliding away under the onslaught of rude editors, temperamental publishers, and nerve-wracking waiting games. Regardless of our frustration level, we must remember that we are Christ's ambassadors in Writer World, and therefore strive to mirror His nature at all times.

Reflecting the character of our Savior is much easier aspired to than accomplished. Focusing on three basic principles can help keep our mirror from cracking.

First, remember your P's and Q's. That's my mother's term for manners. Respect is the bottom line. In Writer World, that would include addressing editors/publishers as Ms. or Mr. until they suggest otherwise. Use proper English and don't assume familiarity before it is developed (although the adorability of your new puppy is important to you, it's doubtful that business contacts will find that subject relevant).

Always verbalize gratitude when anyone takes the time to help you from the lowliest secretary to the CEO. Saying thank you doesn't cost you anything, but *not* expressing thanks can dearly cost the One whom you represent.

I once sent a bouquet of thank you balloons to a high profile person who was kind enough to endorse my first book. She was impressed that Christians were "uncommonly nice", and the groundwork was laid for future spiritual inroads.

Beware of taking up too much time when corresponding. People appreciate your consideration of their busyness, so convey voice messages in thirty seconds or less, expressing yourself clearly and concisely. Always leave your name and number to spare them the trouble of hunting it down. If someone sounds like they're in a hurry, acknowledge that you don't want to inconvenience them, but offer a choice of alternative times to call back: "Would Wednesday morning or afternoon be better?"

When e-mailing, ask before attaching documents (many are not accepted and sending one before obtaining permission may be considered impertinent). Use an appropriate subject line and *never* fudge just to gain audience. Be as brief as possible and remember white space on a page is considerably more reader friendly than wall-to-wall words.

Keep integrity of words and deeds on the forefront of your reputation. Always do what you say and say what you do. Avoid criticizing others. Blowing out someone else's candle doesn't make yours—and certainly not Jesus'—shine brighter. In a business where words *are* the business, it's easy to let our tongues wag a little too loosely and allow gossip to become second nature.

"Don't bad-mouth each other, friends. It's God's Word...that takes a beating in that kind of talk. You're supposed to be honoring the Message, not writing graffiti all over it" (James 4: 11, TM).

Lastly, maintain a sense of humor about mistakes. Hey, everyone knows errors are inevitable, so don't sully your reputation by denying them. Most folks will join in when you laugh at your own faux pas'.

Because I failed to thoroughly proofread a cover letter, instead of assuring an editor that I'm an *internationally* published freelance writer who shuns *incompetence*, I admitted that I'm internally published and try to avoid incontinence.

When I realized my alteration, I hastily apologized and translated that I *meant* that I write from my heart and clean up after myself. The editor chuckled. My article was accepted.

Whether we're dealing with Christians or non-believers in Writer World, our awareness of attitudes

184

and behavior that may become faith stumbling blocks is essential. We want to leave 'em grinning not sinning.

Prayer: *Lord, help us to always remember that discrediting ourselves discredits Christ if we bear His name and reflection. Make us building blocks of faith— never stumbling blocks. Amen.*

Reflection

So how *would* you respond in the opening scenario? How *should* you respond?

Name three areas in which you struggle to *not* lose your temper when frustration overwhelms you. Would you consider these stumbling blocks to others?

List at least two ways you reflect Christ's integrity in your writing life.

"Many believe—and I believe—that I have been designated for this work by God. In spite of my old age, I do not want to give it up; I work out of love for God, and I put all my hope in Him." ~Michelangelo, Italian painter and sculptor (1475-1564)

Excerpt from "Pushing Through the Pain of Publishing"

"After carefully studying Sally Stuart's *Christian Writer's Marketing Guide*, I mailed query letters to thirteen publishers. Within six months, I'd received thirteen rejection letters. I was tempted to abort the process, but God kept reminding me, 'You only need one yes to bring this dream to life, Shannon! Don't give up!' Following the advice of a mentor, I submitted my manuscript to a literary agent, who believed in my message enough to take it to WaterBrook Press, where I finally got that 'yes'!" ~Shannon Etheridge, best-selling author of the *Every Woman's Battle* series and the *Loving Jesus Without Limits* series, www.shannonetheridge.com

"Use real-life illustrations freely. People see themselves in stories." ~Dr. Gary Chapman, Ph.D., best-selling author of *The Five Love Languages*, www.garychapman.org

"Let your hook always be cast; in the pool where you least expect it, there will be a fish." ~Ovid, Roman poet, considered the master of the elegiac couplet (43 B.C.-A.D. 17)

"More writers fail because they give up than because they can't write. Perseverance is one of the most necessary tools a writer can learn." ~Gayle Roper, bestselling author of *A Woman and Her Emotions,* www.gayleroper.com

Just Keep Trying

Suzanne Woods Fisher

"Therefore we do not lose heart. Though outwardly we are wasting away, yet inwardly we are being renewed day by day. For our light and momentary troubles are achieving for us an eternal glory that far outweighs them all. So we fix our eyes not on what is seen, but on what is unseen. For what is seen is temporary, but what is unseen is eternal" (2 Corinthians 4:16-18, NIV).

Simon gave up too easily. He had been fishing hard all night long with only a few measly fish to show for it. He and his partners, James and John, the sons of Zebedee, went back to shore, tired and discouraged, pulled in their nets, and started to pack up the tools of their trade for another day.

Surrounded by a crowd of people, Jesus had been standing by the lake and noticed the boats. He asked Simon if he could teach from the boat. To appease Him, Simon put the boat out into the water a little distance from the shore so Jesus could have a little breathing room for His lessons.

Afterwards, in a touching sign of lavish generosity, Jesus asked Simon to "Put out into deep water, and let down the nets for a catch" (Luke 5:4). Imagine what went through Simon's mind: *Look, Jesus, the fish, if there are any to be found, aren't biting today. I just cleaned and stored my nets and tools for another day. I'll have to start all over again.* Still, Simon liked this Jesus fellow and decided to oblige him. "Because you say so, I will let down the nets" (Luke 5:5).

You can guess the rest of the story. The nets were so full that they had to call in another boat and then the boats were so full of slippery, gasping fish that they *both* began to sink!

What if Simon had refused Jesus' offer? What if he had decided to keep his tools locked up and out of sight? Stored safely away, waiting for a better day to fish? What if Simon had limited Jesus?

Recently, I had an experience like Simon's. I had written an article that I felt was well-edited and full of impact, but it was rejected by all of the magazines for which I usually wrote. Discouraged, I thought of one more venue to try. An unlikely candidate, too. In fact, not only was it a prestigious magazine, but they did almost everything in-house, rarely accepting freelance work.

As I stood at the mailbox, opening the lid to insert the envelope, I ran an objection past the Lord one more time. "God, do you realize that this magazine is probably going to reject the article like all of the others?" And yet, I felt His prompting to keep trying. Just keep at it.

With a thud, I heard the envelope slip down and land at the bottom of the mail container.

One week later, the editor contacted me with an enthusiastic acceptance. He made very few changes in the article and had already scheduled it for publication. Better still, a working relationship developed between us that has resulted in more accepted submissions. My boat felt full to the point of sinking!

Prayer: *Today, Lord, I give You my leaky boat, my discouraged frame of mind, my bum luck at fishing. You ask me to get out my unused nets, unspool them, and put out into deep water. Why would You ask that? I was just out there. I came back with empty nets and a dose of discouragement. But You asked, and by faith, I will try again. Forgive me for quitting too soon, for limiting You. Lord, sometimes I just need to try again. Today, by faith, I need to remember to look to You to fill my nets. Amen.*

Reflection

Can you think of a time recently when you gave up too easily? What did you learn from that experience?

What did it teach you about God? What do you think God wants you to expect from Him?

"Call to me, and I will answer you, and I will tell you great and mighty things, which you do not know" (Jeremiah 33:3, NAS).

Giving Up

"Feel like giving up? Go ahead. Every writer gives up from time to time. I give up all the time. Sometimes I give up after a book reviewer writes a criticism about my work, especially when he or she has clean missed the point. I give up every time an editor sends me a letter with his or her comments about my latest brilliant and flawless work. I give up when the cat looks at me wrong. I give up when I see the industry changing or a badly written book is heralded as a literary wonder. Yup, I give up a lot. Then I turn on my computer, sit down and do the thing I was made to do and love to do. And I keep on doing it until I give up again."
~Alton Gansky, author of *Zero-G*, www.altongansky.com

"Sometimes failure is an awesome teacher. For me, that's meant that I'm realizing once again that I am a writer—at the core. Rejections and disappointments may be a part of the game, but they're not the whole kit and caboodle. I love to work with words, to share what God has done in my life, and to be creative. It fills something in my soul that nothing else can. So of course I will keep writing...and the rest is gravy!" ~Dena Dyer, author of *The Groovy Chicks' Road Trip to Love*, www.denadyer.typepad.com

Writing Tips

1. Read everything you write aloud. Especially dialogue.

2. Keep pen and paper with you at all times. You never know when inspiration will hit...or when you'll be stuck in traffic.

3. Make a scene feel "complete" by ending it with dialogue (internal or external or action from your viewpoint character.

~Sandy Tritt, author of *Everything I Know*, editor, www.InspirationForWriters.com

"Words are only words if we do not breathe our heart into them and bring them to life. A book may be flawlessly written and still be completely dead. And while it still needs to be well-written, an occasional lapse from perfectionism will be willingly overlooked—perhaps even unnoticed—by the reader if the story is heartfelt and full of life." ~Delia Latham, author of *Almost Like A Song* and *Goldeneyes*, www.delialatham.com

"A good writer knows that cutting the flab adds muscle and reduces the fat in his manuscript." ~DiAnn Mills, author of *A Texas Legacy Christmas,* www.diannmills.com

Section 4: Getting "It" Right: The Proper Perspective

"I had just finished my first-ever radio interview. My friend, Jeanne's, advice to breathe proved helpful, though I didn't do the proposed heavy breathing technique. So I chatted with Detroit folks on their way to work on a soon-to-be snowy day.

Right before I called the station, I prayed. And then it hit me. All this publicity stuff and marketing is an opportunity to share Jesus with people. Peace came then. Being on the radio wasn't a venue to be nervous and worry about what I would say, but a time to rely on the Holy Spirit so He could breathe encouraging and redemptive words through me.

This change in perspective helped me tremendously. And it helped me to welcome publicity, not in an ego sense, but in the potential it has to reach more people with news of Jesus." ~Mary E. DeMuth, author of *Building the Christian Family You Never Had,* www.relevantprose.com

"Work to become, not to acquire." ~Unknown

Blessed by Mighty Mites

Debora M. Coty

"Remember that our Lord Jesus said, 'More blessings come from giving than from receiving'" (Acts 20:35, CEV).

"Swell," I monotoned with all the enthusiasm of fresh roadkill. "I can almost buy lunch with this." I held up my paycheck for a whopping $20.15, the compensation I'd just received for an article I'd written—ironically—about persevering to become a successful writer.

"Yep, as long as you skip dessert!" Spouse cheerfully chimed in. "And just think how delighted God will be with your $2 tithe!"

My tithe? Why, I hadn't even considered offering God such a pittance. Come to think of it, I'd been writing "on the side" for a year, and it had never occurred to me to tithe my paltry writing income in addition to my regular salary. Donating $5 here and $10 there just seemed like a raindrop in the proverbial sea.

Then I remembered the story of the widow's mite in Mark 12:41-44. I'm sure she wondered if contributing her two pennies was worth walking all the way to the temple, but Jesus heralded her as our model for selfless giving.

Okay, I thought with new resolve. *If Jesus thinks my mites are valuable, then my mites He'll have.*

My tithe (one tenth of my income as described in Deuteronomy 14:22) that first year for ten published

195

articles totaled about $270. I decided to round it off to $300 and began asking the Lord where He wanted to use it. Within a week, I had my answer.

Over dinner, a friend who teaches deaf education shared with me her efforts to help a teenager who had overcome innumerable obstacles to become the first ever in his poor immigrant family to graduate high school. Besides his profound hearing impairment, Pedro had a severe facial disfigurement for which my friend had located a physician willing to donate treatment. Pedro longed to attend college, but it was unlikely, for he worked long hours in a restaurant kitchen after school to afford the basics that his parents could not provide for his younger siblings.

I sensed that God had arranged our conversation. I asked my friend to deliver my offering to Pedro with an anonymous note praising him for his diligence in obtaining an education and asking God to bless his efforts in pursuing his life goals.

Pedro was astounded that a total stranger would give him what he perceived as a fortune. Moved to tears, he sent a thank you note by my friend to his "Angel from God." Treasuring his heartfelt words, I understood that my mites really were raindrops, small individually, but together they flowed as a mighty outpouring of God's grace and mercy.

The following year, God directed my mighty mites to a disabled, unemployed woman. When she visited my church, I noticed her rubbing her eyes and squinting at her Bible. My mites were able to purchase a pair of much needed bifocals with enough left over for her to pay a few overdue bills. Meeting her physical needs in the Lord's name introduced her to our Savior in a tangible way. She's been a regular front row church attendee since.

When I recently received word that my cousin was involved in a career-ending accident, I knew where my mighty mites were heading for this year.

A hymn title from my childhood serves as my prayer for the love of God to flow through my writing tithes: "Make me a Channel of Blessing," by Harper G. Smyth. And the blessing I receive when I give far outweighs that of the receiver. After all, giving isn't about those who receive; it's about the giver becoming more like our God who gives abundantly.

I'm reminded of the parable of the talents in Matthew 25:21, when the master said to his servant, "You have been faithful in handling this small amount, so now I will give you many more responsibilities" (NLT).

Could our Master Editor be speaking to us writers?

We just never know what future best-seller tithes God may have us in training for now! What a privilege that God provides wordsmiths the honor of extra giving by bestowing on us this special gift.

How about you, fellow writer and generator of mighty mites? "Each of you must make up your own mind about how much to give. But don't feel sorry that you must give and don't feel that you are forced to give. God loves people who love to give," (2 Corinthians 9:7, CEV).

Prayer: *Lord, help us focus on becoming cheerful thanks-givers instead of complacent thanks-getters. Use our writing mites in a mighty way to become channels of blessing to someone today. Amen.*

Reflection

Have you been tithing your writing mites? Why or why not?

Who are two people for whom you might become a channel of blessing with your mighty mites?

List five ways God has blessed you through your writing ministry (not necessarily monetarily). How can you creatively return to Him a portion of your blessing?

"Learn to view rejection simply as an occupational hazard. Persevere through all those rejection slips like jockeys deal with horse-poo. Step over the piles, wipe the nasty off your boots, and keep moving forward." - Debora M. Coty, author of *Everyday Hope* www.DeboraCoty.com

"Do you know how a writer and a flock of geese are alike? They both have a higher calling." ~DiAnn Mills, author of *Awaken My Heart*, www.diannmills.com

"All of us are creating things that are derivative—we're all building on the books we've read, the authors we've admired, and the wisdom we've received." ~Chip MacGregor, agent, MacGregor Literary Agency

Excerpt from "A Writer's Prayer"

"Lord, I know that as I write this book—a book that won't be published for many months—even now, you are preparing hearts that will one day read my words. So let every word I write accurately reflect your truth and your precepts. Supernaturally imbue my writing with that quality that, by your spirit, will woo souls to you." ~Deborah Raney, author of *The Clayburn Novels*, www.deborahraney.com

"One constant battle we have as writers is against professional envy. Ask God to keep your heart pure with an ability to rejoice in the successes of others—even when your successes may not seem as great. God has each of us on our own path. As long as you are staying true to your path, you will find success." ~Ginger Kolbaba, Editor of "Today's Christian Woman" magazine, co-author of *Desperate Pastors' Wives*, www.gingerkolbaba.com

Taming the Green-Eyed Monster
Joanna Bloss

"For wherever there is jealousy and selfish ambition, there you will find disorder and evil of every kind" (James 3:16, NLT).

King Saul had it all. As king of Israel he had wealth, power and any woman he desired. But Saul died a miserable man, and his undoing was entirely his own doing. Saul's problem? Jealousy. He was fiercely envious of a young boy named David—a man after God's own heart.

Being a powerful, wealthy king wasn't enough for Saul. Apparently he didn't want anyone else to have anything remotely as good as he did. Saul spent much of his life pursuing and trying to kill David, and it ultimately killed him.

We've all been on the giving and receiving ends of jealousy, the Green-Eyed Monster. The book of James wisely notes that when jealousy and selfish ambition show up in our lives, disorder and evil are sure to follow.

Unfortunately, professional jealousy seems to be inevitable for writers. That little twinge I feel when I read a rave review about an emerging author's debut release? That's jealousy. The critical spirit that rears its ugly head when I hear someone has just published her fourteenth novel? Nothing but envy. Even though the recipients of my jealousy neither know (or likely care) that I'm feeling the way I do, I have found that the Green-Eyed Monster certainly does me more harm than good.

What to do? Here are some truths I remind myself when I'm overcome with jealousy towards other writers:

There's enough good stuff to go around. Fortunately, there doesn't seem to be a finite number of publishing contracts in existence. When a newbie author gets a manuscript published and I don't, it doesn't mean that I never will. As long as a magazine is in publication, it will continue to need articles; book publishers will continue to produce books as long as there are readers to buy them. The fact that others are getting published should be an encouragement to me that the market for new material is thriving.

The successes of others should be inspirational. Hearing or reading about the publishing successes of other authors can be depressing—or it can be inspiring. It all depends on my perspective. When I hear the Cinderella story of a waitress-turned-prolific-author, I try to let that serve to inspire me to work hard and get my material in circulation. I ask myself what I can learn from the stories of others...what did they do right? How did they get their foot in the door? Is there wisdom I can glean and apply to my own situation?

Jealousy is an ugly word. God hates it when we are jealous of one another. Our jealousy implies that we don't trust Him to give us good gifts, it diminishes the successes of others, and it leads to other destructive feelings like bitterness, resentment, and untruthfulness.

When jealous feelings rise to the surface of my heart, I've found it useful to ask myself why I'm feeling the way I do. Is it because I'm not trusting God? Because I don't want others to succeed? Do I fear I'm not good enough? Jealousy is often the symptom of a greater problem, and figuring out its source can be a critical step in eliminating it altogether.

Saul's jealousy toward David created problems—for both of them. Can you imagine how much nicer the story would have ended if Saul had found himself a good therapist and taken the time to address the root of his feelings? Perhaps he could have learned some things from David—things that would have greatly enriched his life.

Don't let jealousy toward other writers rob you of an opportunity to become a better writer *and* a better person.

Prayer: *Heavenly Father, forgive me for jealous feelings that I've harbored in my heart. I know these feelings do not honor You. Help me to remember that Your blessings are abundant and that You promise good things to those who are faithful to You. Amen.*

Reflection

Is there a particular writer or author of whom you are jealous?

What is at the source of your jealousy?

How does it help to remember that God has enough blessings to share with you, too?

Who Coined "The Green-Eyed Monster"?

"O beware, my lord, of jealousy!
It is the green-eyed monster which doth mock
The meat it feeds on."
~William Shakespeare (1564 - 1616), "Othello", Act 3 scene 3

Although jealousy was already alive and well by the time of William Shakespeare (who can forget Cain & Abel?), he may have been the one to coin the term "green-eyed monster." He refers to old green eyes in both *The Merchant of Venice* and *Othello*.

"Why be envious of other writers? I must believe God has a message inside this container of clay that only I can write. I ask God to replace jealousy with trust. I do trust in His plan, His will, and His purpose for me." ~Donna Shepherd, author of *Topsy Turvy Land*, www.donnajshepherd.com

The Written Word

"Holds a thought on a page
like a seed.
Waits to settle
into a fertile heart,
to produce a bountiful crop
in heaven's kingdom."
~Sally Jadlow, author of *The Late Sooner*, www.sallyjadlow.com

"The quote that got me writing in the first place is from noted author Jane Valentine Barker: 'Jeanne, if you don't write this down, it'll be lost forever. Get going!' So I did, and now I have my novel *Lavinia* as a reality." ~Jeanne Wilde, author of *Lavinia*

"One of the things I have to be careful of when writing, because I write for mostly Christian markets, is that my daily work and Bible research is not my devotional time. Sometimes it's easy to run the two together. I still need that personal quiet time before God. It helps me to be a better writer!" ~Jennie Hilligus, contributor to *A Cup of Comfort: Book of Prayer*

Promoting Yourself
Suzanne Woods Fisher

"Publish His glorious acts throughout all the earth..."(Psalm 96:3, TLB).

When Timothy was a young pastor keeping the church of Ephesus on track, Paul wrote him a letter. Two, in fact. Filled with pastoral advice, there's a lovely, underlying message that keeps bubbling up to the surface.

Paul's motive in writing was to encourage Timothy to stay the course, to not let others intimidate him because of his age, to remember the great work God had ahead of him. It seemed as if Timothy was a talented, capable young man who didn't know that he was very talented or very capable. But Paul certainly did. At one point, he urged Timothy: "For God did not give us a spirit of timidity, but a spirit of power, of love and of self-discipline...I pray that you...may be filled to the measure of all the fullness of God" (2 Timothy 1:7, NIV).

One of the hardest aspects of being a writer is embracing the need to promote oneself. Self-promoting feels so...so...un-Christ like. Most writers are not flaming

203

extroverts; we're more the reflective sort who process our thoughts through the written word. We're the Timothys of the Paul-and-Timothy duo. Hopefully, we have some Pauls in our life who can give us the encouragement we need *when* we need it.

One friend struggled with the expectation of the publishing house to promote herself after her first book was published. When the publisher recommended that she contact radio stations to try and schedule author-interviews for herself, she shuddered.

"Linda," he reasoned, "you wrote a book that is meant to glorify God. How can you do that if you don't publicize your book?" The publisher made a good point. I could relate to Linda's reluctance. When I signed a contract for my first novel, the publisher asked me to set up a website to start developing a reader base months before the book would be published. She also recommended that I start a blog (lingo for web log).

I created the website but then I didn't let anyone know about it for months. I felt too self-conscious. Finally, I took the plunge and sent the url to some friends, who sent it to their friends. Same for the blog. To my surprise, both blog and website were easier to create and more fun than I had expected. The blog, kind of an on-line journal, has been a place to share my faith. I've considered it to be a near-daily writing exercise, like piano scales, to sharpen my skills. And a plus: it's all without the need of an editor's approval!

If God has called us to this work, and we believe that we are working to glorify Him, we need to put aside our own insecurities and false sense of modesty and do what we can to get our work to the public. That may include hosting your own website, keeping up a blog, asking bookstore managers for book signings, calling radio stations for author interviews.

It might mean being bold enough to ask other authors for endorsements. One editor at a writing conference even suggested offering to prepare an endorsement for an author and to ask permission to ascribe him credit. In other words, to market yourself. Just remember, the focus isn't self-glorification. The end result is to glorify the God whom we serve.

Prayer: *Lord Jesus, help me to be more like Timothy who, despite age and insecurities, carefully guarded all that had been entrusted to him (1 Timothy 1:19; 6:30). Amen.*

Reflection

Does the idea of promotion make you wince? Do you dread the thought? Why or why not?

How can you pray to be released from wrong thinking about promotion and be renewed by the right thinking about it?

Magazines & Newsletters

"One of the absolute best things you can do is to work on your craft of writing with shorter forms. Books are long—I know not very profound but true. Magazine articles and newsletters and other forms of writing are much shorter, the publication lead time is less, and they are much more achievable. There are too many writers who are stuck on submitting their long manuscript and never work on magazine articles. It's a shame." ~Terry Whalin, agent, Whalin Literary Agency

Writer's Block

"I stand up, stretch, sit down, and start banging on the keys. If the prose is awful, I can edit it later, but the fact is, I have to write myself out of it. I also remind myself why I'm writing and whose approval I seek." ~Liz Curtis Higgs, Christian humorist, author of 26 books, including her best-selling *Bad Girls of the Bible* series, www.lizcurtishiggs.com

"Marketing is a significant part of establishing your writing career. You have to work hard to get yourself known. It will often feel like it's you against everyone else out there, but you're not alone. You have to stay on top of everything in order to keep up with the competition. Most importantly, don't lose hope. Stay connected, but don't overwhelm yourself. Only you know what you can handle, and you can only do your best not someone else's. Work to your strengths, and eventually, the payoff will come." ~Amber Miller, author of *Quills & Promises*, www.ambermiller.com

"Use your time away from the keyboard to create scenes in your head so that when you sit down to write, the ideas are ready to flow. (My best thoughts come while doing menial chores like washing dishes.)" ~Michelle Buckman, author of *Maggie Come Lately,* www.michellebuckman.com

You Mean I Paid for This?

Faith Tibbetts McDonald

"Have I not commanded you? Be strong and courageous. Do not be terrified; do not be discouraged, for the Lord your God will be with you wherever you go" (Joshua 1:9, NIV).

With high hopes that participating in a writers' conference would ignite my writing career, I attended my first conference. I brought two manuscripts to the conference. Manuscript One: a children's story. I thought—humbly, of course—that editors would spout superlatives regarding its stellar qualities and stumble over each other as they rushed to purchase the rights to publish this eventual best seller.

Manuscript Two: a piece written from my heart on how busy moms could connect with God regularly. I doubted any editor would even read that piece.

When the conference was over, I left with three written critiques in hand. One editor's critique revealed that she hadn't read more than the first page of my children's story, and she found no reason to go on. She wrote that the story was void of promise.

After that blow, wondering why I had even bothered to submit, I braced myself for the agony of reading the comments regarding the less promising work which two editors had read and critiqued. Both editors accepted it for publication.

And so I entered the bewildering writers' conferences world where my highest writing hopes have been dashed...and developed. Over the years, I've gleaned four must-have qualities to enable a writer to survive, maybe even to thrive, at a conference.

Resilience: Every time I attend a writers' conference, at least one editor (sometimes more) is willing and able to find more things wrong than right with my work. The editor who read my first attempt at a book proposal brusquely declared, "I can't imagine anyone, anywhere wanting to read this. And it's not funny at all." (I had billed the work as a humorous piece.) Later in my room, tears coursed down my cheeks, and I contemplated packing up and heading home.

At times like this, I've learned to hold fast to my calling. I remember that God has called me to write, and I review Bible verses that confirm that calling. One of my favorites: "The Sovereign Lord has given me an instructed tongue, to know the word that sustains the weary" (Isaiah 50:4).

Resilience in difficulties and the act of carrying on despite disappointment reveals character. When the response to my writing disappoints me, I ask God to strengthen my resilience. He always answers that prayer.

When I feel disappointed, it's easy to surmise (especially in the excited chatter about potential publication that characterizes a writers' conference) that I'm the only author dealing with rejection. I've learned that emotional letdown is part of everyone's experience. It's something we must cope with.

Discernment: An appreciation for a manuscript is based on an editor's personal taste. I've learned to ask,

"What can I do to make this better?" If I understand and agree with the editor's suggestions, I implement them.

People of varying credentials and ability attend writers' conferences—many are willing to offer suggestions on how to get published. I've learned to listen to varying viewpoints and then pray for specific guidance for my career. Sometimes, the options and unsolicited advice overwhelm me, but God promises to lead even when the way is bewildering (Isaiah 42:16).

Expectation for God to work: The truth is that my expectations have never been fulfilled at a writers' conference. The part of me that believes in fairy tales yearns to be discovered and catapulted to best-seller status every time I attend a conference. However, I've learned to set aside my agenda. As soon as I do, God does more than I can ask or imagine. Opportunities fall in my lap. I meet caring Christian people who've become my friends and encouragers.

Confidence: Connecting with like-minded people is a positive aspect of conferences. Yet the arena in which that connection is forged intimidates me. In the writers' conference bustle, it seems every writer is more creative, well-spoken, and confident than I am. Some editors and agents exude arrogance. The competition for editors' attention is intense.

It would be easy to be cowed in a corner and venture out only to grab a cup of coffee; however, I have learned to approach seminars, round table discussions, and editorial consults in the confidence God provides. He has filled me with the desire to write. He will provide the opportunities. God is with me.

Prayer: *Father, thank You that I am not here alone. Thank You that although the atmosphere is intimidating You will enable* *me to confidently present my ideas clearly when the opportunity opens up. Open my eyes to encourage another writer who is even more insecure than I feel. Amen.*

Reflection

What Bible verse confirms your calling to write?

List three things you expect to happen at your next writers' conference. Are these your expectations or God's? How can you put aside your expectations and hopes and allow for God's guidance?

Tips to Survive a Writers' Conference:

"Be a sponge.
Don't be shy.
Be polite.
Take advantage.
Pace yourself.
Be realistic."
~Faith Tibbetts McDonald, freelance writer

Remember that it is normal to...

"Get discouraged.
Cry.
To see unexpected doors open.
Change your writing goals.
Lose perspective.
Find that God is working in your heart about something that is completely unrelated to writing." ~
from Mt. Hermon's 2006 Writers' Conference, written by Jeannette Hanscome

"Be willing to invest in your career. Invest your time, your energy, your talent, and your money. Build your platform and connect it to the world through a professional website. I am convinced that I would not have landed the book contracts I landed without a professional website. Hands down the best investment I made!" ~Trish Berg, author of *Rattled* and *The Great American Supper Swap*, www.trishberg.com

Excerpt from "Pushing Through the Pain of Publishing"

"When you hold that first published book in your hands, it's like holding a beautiful newborn baby in your arms for the first time. That little miracle looks like you, it sounds like you, and the joy of beholding it makes all the pain completely worthwhile!" ~Shannon Etheridge, best-selling author of *Every Woman's Battle* series and the *Loving Jesus Without Limits* series, www.shannonetheridge.com

"We can write words, but only God can touch hearts through our words. That's why it's important to pray for our readers." ~Lydia E. Harris teaches "Empower Your Writing Through Prayer" at writers' conferences, www.lydiaeharris.com

Developing Camel Knees

Debora M. Coty

"Keep on praying" (1 Thessalonians 5:17, NLT).

James, author of the epistle and half-brother of Jesus (son of Mary and Joseph), was nicknamed "Old Camel Knees," because of calluses he developed while kneeling in prayer (recorded in A.D. 325 by Eusebius of Caeserea in an account of church history).

Kneeling is out of vogue in many modern day Christian circles, but when space and bum knees permit, I find it's the best position to get my heart in the right perspective for prayer—it reflects an attitude of submission, humbleness, and earnest supplication. I can't think of any better summarization of my feelings when I'm preparing a manuscript for submission.

Because I view my writing as a ministry, I pray daily for my work to honor the Minister of that ministry. I pause by the mailbox with each and every outgoing manuscript and lift the parcel to the Lord as an offering, asking for His blessing upon my work.

Before clicking *send*, I pray for His will to be done with this query or manuscript and ask for strength to view rejections simply as closed doors meant to guide me along the corridor to the opened door He has waiting for me. My husband once walked in to find me with one hand on the monitor screen and the other lifted heavenward. He asked when I had started worshiping my computer.

Three little words: *Keep on praying.* Yet it's one of the most powerful verses in the Bible; a scripture that Christian writers, above all, should heed as our personal mandate. But what exactly is the function of prayer? How does it work? Can we really influence the Creator of all things by our simple petition?

For centuries, religious scholars have pondered those questions and come to the conclusion that this side of heaven, we'll never truly understand how or why prayer works. All we know for sure is that throughout His word, God repeatedly tells us to pray.

Prayer is not just spiritual punctuation; it's every word of our life story.

My favorite analogy of prayer is a magnifying lens. Picture a child standing in a sunny field holding a magnifying glass over a blade of grass. A wisp of smoke ascends from the spot where a superheated sunbeam is trained on the blade. Soon a flame erupts, and the grass begins to blaze. The lens serves as a focal point for the broad rays of the sun to exponentially increase their potency into a powerful beam.

Prayer, in the same way, reins in the broad *attention* of God to focus His supernatural power on a specific area.

We must, however, resist the temptation to view prayer as a free pass to success. Praying over our work doesn't necessarily mean that editors and publishers will be lining up at our door. The Almighty does not provide "golden Midas touch" tickets or "skip to the head of the line" coupons because we followed the magical formula in asking for them.

But we shouldn't rule out God working behind the scenes to provide answers to prayer in unexpected ways!

After five long months of intense prayer while communicating with a publishing house editor about a book proposal, I was devastated to suddenly receive a standardized rejection notice with no explanation. What happened? Had my prayer magnifying glass shattered? Was God answering "No," or simply "Wait"?

A sleepless night on my camel knees galvanized me to become proactive.

I e-mailed the editor a brief note thanking her for her time and encouragement, asking if she would be kind enough to share what had gone wrong and suggest manuscript improvements for pursuit of publication elsewhere. Within ten minutes she responded that the problem wasn't my writing; they had two similar books in their line and couldn't add another at this time.

But that wasn't all! She asked if I'd consider a book project for which she needed a writer with just my style.

Now isn't that just like God?

Prayer: *Heavenly Father, thank You for the gift of prayer—that mysterious, unexplainable nerve that innervates the muscles of Your all-powerful hands. Help us as writers yielded to Your service to develop camel knees by our commitment to keep on praying! Amen.*

Reflection

Do you view your writing as a ministry? Why or why not? How does this perspective affect your approach and work habits?

What is the function of prayer in your writing career?

Name three answered prayers (yes, no, or wait a while) that were instrumental in determining the path of your writing career.

So You Landed a Book Contract

"So you landed a book contract. You thought you had finally ascended the Mt. Everest of the publishing process. You haven't. Or rather, there's another, yet steeper mountain that you must climb once you deposit your advance at the bank." ~Dave Goetz, author of *How to Keep the Suburbs from Killing your Soul,* www.davegoetz.com

So You Landed a Book Contract (continued)

"It's called Mt. Publicity. It's a mountain that is hidden by the first one. You thought your publisher did all that marketing and publicity stuff. All you needed to do was to write the book, look good for the publicity shots, and put together a few talking points for your interviews. And then wait for the royalties to fund your summer cottage on Lake Michigan." ~Dave Goetz, author of *How to Keep the Suburbs from Killing your Soul,* www.deathbysuburb.net

So You Landed a Book Contract (continued)

"You thought that great writing sells itself. It doesn't. Great writing is, well, great writing. That's it." ~Dave Goetz, author, *How to Keep the Suburbs from Killing your Soul,* www.davegoetz.com

So You Landed a Book Contract (continued)

"Here's the reality of book publishing: Your publisher is as lost as you are about how to sell your book. It doesn't matter the size of your publisher. These days, few publishers understand the new realities of marketing in the Age of Clutter. In the Age of 50,000 New Books Published Each Year." ~Dave Goetz, author of *How to Keep the Suburbs from Killing your Soul*, www.davegoetz.com

So You Landed a Book Contract (continued)

"Only Paris Hilton has seemed to figure out how to stay in front and center of the media. So if you're not Ms. Hilton, what can you do? You start with these four core ideas:

Don't blow your advance by paying off your credit cards or taking a trip to Jackson Hole. Use that money as risk capital. Use that money to promote your book. In short, invest in the success of your own book. Spend your advance wisely on cost-effective, smart publicity. That's thinking long-term." (to be continued, next chapter) ~Dave Goetz, author of *How to Keep the Suburbs from Killing your Soul*, www.davegoetz.com

"Others may not take you seriously until they see your name in print in some national publication, but as long as you are writing, you are a writer." ~Michelle Buckman, author of *Maggie Come Lately*, www.michellebuckman.com

Groundhog Day

Suzanne Woods Fisher

"Your grace is sufficient for me, because your power is made perfect in my weakness" (2 Cor. 12:9, NIV).

In the movie *Groundhog Day*, weatherman Bill Murray finds himself repeating the same day over and over again. Finally, he "gets it"— the perspective that he has been sorely lacking. And the clock moves forward.

Wouldn't it be nice if time could stop until we really "get it" about a core issue? "Get" the perspective that God wants us to have? Then we could move on, never to revisit it. But life doesn't work that way. Instead, that core issue pops up again and again, as if God is saying wearily, "Okay...let's try this one more time."

Core issues need to be dealt with. In the book of Acts, the question of whether believing Gentiles should comply to Jewish tradition nearly unhinged the young church. What may seem obvious to our modern ears was anything *but* obvious to first century believers. The real question wasn't about tradition; it faced the issue of whether Jesus' death and resurrection was enough to provide salvation. *Talk about a core issue!*

Paul knew the answer lay in Christ alone. With godly wisdom, he reunited the early church at the defining Jerusalem Council (Acts 15). The apostle Peter

217

witnessed and affirmed Paul's direction for the church. Not long after, however, Peter slipped back into an emphasis on Jewish tradition (Galatians 2). Only after receiving a thorough upbraiding by Paul did Peter truly "get it." *God's perspective.*

Peter, Peter, Peter. So quick to jump to conclusions. So impulsive. So sure of his own opinions. So slow to ask for counsel. *When* would he ever learn?

"Ahem," God politely coughs.

When will *I* ever learn?

Recently, I received a disappointing "no" from a publisher for a book deal. I can handle rejection; I've developed a tough hide. But when I asked for helpful feedback, the response was, "It was good writing but not extraordinary."

Not extraordinary? Not special? Those words cut deep into the heart of a writer. They felt so personal.

That evening, I complained to the Lord, telling Him all about my feelings of continually striving but never arriving. "I'm just not as far along as I hoped I'd be. Sometimes I feel as if I'm right back where I started—again," I wailed. Not unlike *Groundhog Day.*

Almost audibly, I sensed His response: "If you don't understand that you are extraordinary simply because you are you, an individual loved by the Almighty God, if you don't 'get that,' then it really doesn't matter how many publishing contracts you will ever land. It will never be enough."

When am I ever going to *get* that core issue settled? As a published author, I know that the good feeling publication can bring is short lived and quickly eclipsed by attention to the next project. Publication doesn't bring the deep down validation that writers assume is waiting for them there. It's *not* like a pot of gold at the end of the rainbow.

In *Bird by Bird: Some Instructions on Writing and Life*, Anne Lamott reflects about her students: "I try to make sure they understand that writing, and even getting good at it, and having books and stories and articles published, will not open the doors that most of them hope for. It will not make them well. It will not give them the feeling that the world has finally validated their parking tickets, that they have in fact finally arrived. My writer friends, and they are legion, do not go around beaming with quiet feelings of contentment. Most of them go around with haunted, abused, surprised looks on their faces, like lab dogs on whom very personal deodorant sprays have been tested."

Christ alone *is* sufficient for me. Like Peter, I need to "get" that concept so it doesn't need to be revisited. No one can take that Truth away from me, either. Not a publisher, not a bad review, not a disgruntled reader.

I am extraordinary not because of anything I do, but because I am His. As are you.

Prayer: *Heavenly Father, thank You for giving me multiple chances to become grounded in this critically important concept. Thank You for assuring me that You are my sole source of validation. Amen.*

Reflection

What do you hope that publication will do for you?

What lesson, specifically in relation to your writing, might God be wanting you to "get"?

Do you ever feel as if the end result, publication, can become too important? Why or why not?

So You Landed a Book Contract (continued)

"In the first three months after the release of your book, do five activities per day to promote your book. 'How can I come up with five per day?' you ask. Set the goal, and your mind will go to work. Call Oprah. Send copies of your book to all the jurors at a major trial. (That's what Jack Canfield, author of *Chicken Soup for the Soul* did. And when the jurors came out of deliberations from the O.J. Simpson trial, the cameras panned to see what the jurors were holding—and voila! The soup began to boil.) The first three months are the most crucial. You must get into orbit. I call the first three months the 'solid rocket booster phase.'" ~Dave Goetz, author of *How to Keep the Suburbs from Killing your Soul,* www.davegoetz.com

So You Landed a Book Contract (continued)

"3. Network before your book releases. The worse time to find a new job is when you desperately need one. The wise job seekers are at work networking with friends and acquaintances before they need a new place of employment. The same is true for promoting your book. Build relationships with key influencers and thought leaders a year or two before your book releases." ~Dave Goetz, author of *How to Keep the Suburbs from Killing your Soul,* www.davegoetz.com

So You Landed a Book Contract (continued)

"4. Be persistent. This aphorism is the most annoying cliché never heeded. After three months, your publicist will stop answering your emails. Your book will suddenly become backlisted. 'Backlisted' is a codeword that your publisher translates as 'Dude, I can't remember your name or any book with a title like that. Are you sure you published with us?'" ~Dave Goetz, author of *How to Keep the Suburbs from Killing your Soul*, www.davegoetz.com

So You Landed a Book Contract (continued)

"But if you stop your efforts now, your book will lose its trajectory and begin an almost vertical descent in sales. I recommend spending less time thinking about your next book and more time conducting activities that maintain or raise the trajectory of the book you've just published." ~Dave Goetz, author of *How to Keep the Suburbs from Killing your Soul*, www.davegoetz.com

So You Landed a Book Contract (conclusion)

"What you really want is not necessarily huge success for this book. What you want is a shot at writing your next one. You need enough sales to make your publisher consider exercising the option in your contract. If you can write a book, you can learn to create buzz for it." ~Dave Goetz, author of *How to Keep the Suburbs from Killing your Soul*, www.davegoetz.com

"When we prepare our hearts and minds with the truth of God's Word, we will be ready to write His answer." ~Susan Kelly Skitt, author of *The One Year Life Verse Devotional,* www.livingtheadventurouslife.blogspot.com

Becoming Temple Caretakers

Debora M. Coty

"We are the temple of the living God" *(2 Corinthians 6:16, NIV).*

Brian groaned as he cradled the phone between his cheek and shoulder. "Oh man, I'm never going to finish this manuscript; I can't feel my fingers," he confessed to his writing buddy, rubbing his hands together. "The numbness in my hands drives me crazy when I type for more than a half hour. They feel dead when I wake up in the mornings, too."

Cindy turned her head toward the monitor wedged into the far left corner of her workspace and winced at the burning sensation in her upper forearm as she stretched her right arm forward to operate her mouse. Due to spatial limitations, she routinely worked with her head turned, elbow fully extended, and her wrist cocked up to reach the mouse. She paused to massage her aching right shoulder and neck.

Brian and Cindy don't realize they're battling an unseen enemy that wreaks more havoc on writing careers than any heartless editor—repetitive strain injuries (RSI). Each year, the insipid RSI beast stalks and devours the wellbeing of millions of unsuspecting typists.

The Bible says our bodies are God's temples. If we as temple caretakers are to withstand battering gales and the onslaught of relentless enemy attacks, we must fortify our living structures from within! Knowledge and prevention are our best defense.

As an occupational therapist specializing in upper extremity orthopedic rehabilitation, I've treated innumerable cases of RSI, or overuse syndrome. Writers who spend prolonged hours at their keyboards are vulnerable to several specific maladies.

Brian, in the previous scenario, shows classic symptoms of carpal tunnel syndrome (CTS), which occurs when the median nerve is pinched at the wrist by chronically poor positioning (bending the wrist to reach a keyboard that is too low), or internal inflammation due to constant finger motion. The median nerve innervates the thumb, index, long, and half the ring finger. Numbness, tingling, or pain from CTS can occur in any or all of these digits. Symptoms are often worse at night or early morning because of our tendency to sleep with our wrists flexed (fetal position), thus impinging the median nerve.

Treatment by an orthopedic physician should be pursued immediately upon onset of symptoms; the earlier treatment begins, the better the chances of avoiding surgery. Frequent flexor stretching (assume praying position palm-to-palm then lower hands to waist) and use of wrist support splints to keep the tunnel open at night are highly recommended. If symptoms persist, splints should be worn while keyboarding also (splints are available at most drug stores and discount department stores).

Cindy has created a whopping case of tennis elbow (lateral epicondylitis) by constantly extending her arm and wrist for mousing. The muscles that straighten the elbow, wrist, and fingers are overstressed, causing pain in the dorsum (the fingernail side) of the forearm. Her first step should be to adjust her table, equipment, and chair position so that her elbows remain at a 90 degree angle at all times, forearms supported, and wrists in neutral position (not cocked up or down to reach the keyboard). All items frequently used (phone, printer, mouse) should be within 15 inches of the body to prevent excessive reaching.

A tennis elbow cuff (reduces muscle friction in the upper forearm) and wrist support splint (keeps the wrist in a neutral position to allow the extensor muscles to rest) may be helpful. Frequent rest breaks and extensor stretching (using opposite hand to gently bend wrist forward with elbow extended) will help ease muscle tension.

Both Brian and Cindy need to alter their ergonomics to prevent tendonitis of neck and shoulder muscles. A headset or speaker phone should be used rather than the phone-on-shoulder technique, and the monitor should be placed at eye level directly in front of the typist.

Paced daily timeouts for a few simple stretching exercises can bring immense relief to tight and painful shoulders: exaggerated shoulder rolls forward and backward, ear-to-shoulder stretches (gently pushing head with opposite hand); chin-to-shoulder stretches (also using opposite hand); chin tucks (push chin back toward Adam's apple), "chicken neck's" (thrust chin forward); and pectoralis stretches (clasp hands behind back, lift).

None of us want our temples to fall into ruins. With a sturdy foundation of proper prevention and a slap or two of maintenance mortar, our flesh and blood cathedrals can glorify God for decades to come.

Prayer: *Master Designer, we want to diligently uphold and preserve these bodies that You've entrusted to us; help us honor You by not allowing one brick of Your temple to crumble from neglect. Amen.*

Reflection

Considering that your body is a temple of God, would you say that your temple currently is in mint condition or in need of repairs or renovation?

Assess your work space; cite two changes that would make your area more ergonomically sensible. Remember, an ounce of prevention is *immensely* better than pounding out a cure!

Take a moment to try the exercises recommended at the end of the devotion; will you commit to take two minutes out of each two hour work period for a well-earned stretch break?

Temple Care

"God wired our bodies to move, not to sit in one place for extended periods of time. Write and fulfill your call, but remember that you're far more than a writer. You are His. Take the time to care for the temple He has given you. Walk, reach, stretch, and rest. Nourish your soul, too. Exercise faith and walk in love. Don't just write for the sake of being a published author; be a writer with a life-message." ~Susie Larson, speaker, author of *Balance that Works when Life Doesn't*, www.susielarson.com

"Satan is a chronic grumbler. The Christian ought to be a living doxology." ~Martin Luther, German monk and church reformer (1483-1546)

Excerpt from "The Downside of Success"

"When we struggle to write and face rejections and setbacks, we learn about ourselves. Isn't it possible that we can learn even more about ourselves as we move into greater levels of success? Maybe the dark of success is something else God wants us to learn." ~Cecil Murphey, best-selling author, speaker, and conference teacher, www.themanbehindthewords.com

"Be sure your narrative and dialogue keep the reader accurately settled in the proper time by checking and rechecking historical facts and by remaining true to the customs and appropriate vocabulary of the times. If the character is a British private in 1776, he won't text message King George in London to say, 'Dude, those guys R n trouble now'." ~Louise M. Gouge, author, *Then Came Faith*, www.louisemgouge.com

Even Editors Need Editors

Suzanne Woods Fisher

"To all perfection I see a limit" (Psalm 119:96, NIV).

In today's world, perfectionism has a bad rap. Think of the modern labels that are slapped on perfectionists: obsessive, compulsive, anal retentive. And *those* are the polite ones.

There are circumstances, though, when perfectionism is not only desired but mandated. Brain surgery, for example. Architecture, for another. And even communication.

Definitely communication. Even though we live in an age when text and instant messaging have reduced words to abbreviated letters while simultaneously glorifying slang. Even in a day when the ability to spell a word correctly without a computer spell-check seems as outdated as a horse and buggy.

God has always taken communication seriously. Just three months into the Exodus from Egypt, He called Moses up to the top of Mount Sinai for a private tutorial. Over the next forty days, Moses was given the Law, designed by God, to shape the Israelites into becoming a people of promise. The mountain was covered with a dense cloud by day and fire by night.

When the Lord finished speaking to Moses on Mount Sinai, He gave him the two tablets of the Testimony. "They were inscribed on both sides, front and back. The tablets were the work of God, the writing was the writing of God, engraved on the tablets" (Exodus 32:15-16, NIV). Chiseled out of stone, created by the very Author of Language, the tablets were a work of perfection. A masterpiece, crafted to last many, many centuries. The words were well-planned, carefully executed, clear, concise, powerful, and yet with an economy of words.

As aspiring writers, we need to strive for excellence in our work. Communicating clearly is a skill, a craft, an art. Like any other skill, it takes time to learn the craft well.

Time is my biggest obstacle in striving for excellence. I've made many mistakes of working in haste, eager to get the project completed. I've sent out work riddled with errors and typos and grammatical problems and syntax issues. And that was *after* I proofed it!

Once, to my chagrin, I remember describing a movie in an article, and the editor wrote back: Had I even *seen* this movie? Gulp. No, I hadn't. I had heard someone describe it, and I didn't double check my facts. I was mortified. It was a telling and lasting lesson. I haven't made that mistake again. I learned the value of developing Argus-eyes—a writer's term for careful proofreading.

Mistakes are part of the learning curve. They're part of being human. Poet Luci Shaw told me a story of the first book published by her husband's brand-new company, Harold Shaw Publishers. They had forgotten to add page numbers. Whoops! They never made that mistake again.

David Kopp, former editor of "Christian Parenting Today" magazine, admitted spelling Ingrid Trobisch's name three different ways throughout a single issue. "We spelled it one way on the cover, another way in the table, and another way on the feature. The one on the feature was correct," he confessed.

His cheeks still flame when he tells the story. But it's a relief to know I'm in good company—even publishers and editors make mistakes.

Still, with modern technological capabilities, it is inexcusable to send in a manuscript with a spelling error (yes, inexcusable, but it happens). Even most grammatical errors are highlighted by computer software. I've heard more than one editor say that expectations have risen in tandem with technology. One publisher recently noted that he's seeing more and more manuscripts arrive at his publishing house already embellished with graphic design. Talk about adding an *oomph* factor!

There are many tools available to aid you in the quest for excellence in your work—books on writing, a friend known for her Argus-eyed proofreading,, conferences, paid editing. Slow down. Take your time. Learn the ins-and-outs of the business. Avoid looking like an amateur simply because you haven't researched the mechanics, say, for example, of writing a query letter or a proposal.

And when you do make a mistake, use it as a learning opportunity to improve your work.

Above all, admonish yourself to write well, whether it is an e-mail, a thank you note, or a synopsis of a debut novel. Not only is the competition too fierce to present less-than-excellent work, but more importantly, we should be writing with a higher objective—to give glory to the very Author of Language, the very first Communicator, who brought forth our world with *His* Living Word.

Prayer: *Giver of Words, let me learn from Your example as a communicator. Plant in me a lifelong desire to use my calling to honor You. Amen.*

Reflection

Can you think of an example where you made a careless writing error that later came back to haunt you? How did it feel then? How does it feel now?

How well do you do at learning from your mistakes? Are you seeing an improvement in this area?

What are three things you can do to ensure a manuscript is completed to the best of your ability before sending it to an editor?

What Does it Mean to Be *Argus-Eyed*?

Argus was a hundred-eyed giant from Greek mythology. Legend has it that after Argus was killed, his eyes were put in the tail of a peacock. When one is called *Argus-eyed*, it means she is watchful, sharp-sighted, and extremely vigilant.

"Eloquent you may be and well-educated as well, however, you'll communicate more effectively with your audience if you write the gutsy or gory or goofy truth just as it is, not dressed up in Sunday clothes that spiff up and cover the reality of your topic." ~Jean E. Syswerda, author of *The Women's Devotional Guide to the Bible,* co-author of the best-selling *Women of the Bible*

"As a Christian, I feel a call to create. I consider it worship to God when I use the talent He's given me." ~Donna Shepherd, author of *Topsy Turvy Land,* www.donnajshepherd.com

"One thing I emphasize with both high school and college creative writing students getting ready to send their work out, is to first get a stockpile of material then develop some type of system for sending it out and keeping track of where you sent it." ~Stacy Gillett Coyle, award-winning poet, *Cloud Seeding*

"It's hard to know when enough is enough—when the book is edited enough, when you've publicized enough, when the cover design is tweaked enough, when you've written enough. At all times, keep an ear to the ground for that beautiful, still voice of The One who called you. Know it intimately so that you can recognize its directive presence in your life." ~Rebeca Seitz, President, Glass Road Public Relations, LLC

Proverbs' Wisdom for Writers

Joanna Bloss

"A word aptly spoken is like apples of gold in settings of silver" (Proverbs 25:11, NIV).

I'm always moved by parents' creativity in communicating wisdom to their children. I remember reading *Letters to Karen* by Charlie Shedd when I was younger and thinking how special it would be to have a whole book of letters written to me by my father.

Then there was the Oprah episode that reduced me to tears. She told the story of a dying mother who created a video journal filled with wisdom for her young daughter to turn to long after her mother was gone. Among many other things, the mother talked about how to wear make-up, gave advice for her daughter's first date, and offered wishes for a happy marriage. Imagine how much that young lady must treasure that priceless gift.

In the Bible, King Solomon did much the same thing for his sons. We call it the Book of Proverbs, but at its core, this little gem is a heartfelt love letter from a father to a son, not only from Solomon to his sons, but from God to us. "My son, if you accept my words and store up my commands within you..." he says, "then you will understand the fear of the Lord and find the knowledge of God " (Proverbs 2:1, 5).

Proverbs is one of my favorite books of the Bible because it contains an abundance of short and sweet sayings that are as relevant to me now as I'm sure they were to Solomon's sons centuries ago. The wisdom of Proverbs applies to every area of my life, including my writing. Here is just a sampling of the wealth of instruction I've gained:

"All hard work brings a profit, but mere talk leads only to poverty" (14:23). Am I a writer, or do I merely talk about wanting to be a writer? Talking about it is easy, but that essentially leads to poverty. The path to becoming a good writer is paved with hard work.

"In his heart a man plans his course, but the Lord determines his steps" (16:9). I may have a career path all laid out for myself and have already made decisions about all I want to accomplish. But when it's all said and done, I'm not the one who is in control of my writing—the Lord is, and He promises direction.

"Whoever gives heed to instruction prospers, and blessed is he who trusts in the Lord" (16:20). How do you feel when someone critiques your work? Uncomfortable? Defensive? Irritated? Trusting God and heeding His instruction (as well as that of others whom you trust) is one of the keys to writing prosperity.

"Stop listening to instruction my son, and you will stray from the words of knowledge" (19:27). In fact, Solomon offers a warning—if we stop listening to the wise instruction of God and others, our words will *not* be wise—we'll stray from Truth, and the results will get ugly.

"Let another praise you, and not your own mouth; someone else, and not your own lips" (27:2). As Christians who write, we may sometimes find ourselves in a precarious position when it comes to self-promotion. I can understand and appreciate the value of marketing my work and possessing confidence when I deal with editors and potential publishers, but I must also recognize the temptation of taking pride in my own abilities. If my motivation is to further my own agenda rather than God's kingdom, my writing (and the marketing of my writing) will inevitably reflect this conflict of interest.

"Pleasant words are a honeycomb, sweet to the soul and healing to the bones" (16:24). This proverb captures much of what I want my writing to be about. I want my words to resonate within my readers' souls, to provide healing, comfort, strength and encouragement. How is this accomplished? Here's the key...

"Trust in the Lord with all your heart and lean not on your own understanding; in all your ways acknowledge Him, and He will make your paths straight" (Proverbs 3:5-6).

Prayer: *Wise Father, thank You for the wisdom Your word provides. Thank You that it is living and active and relevant to every situation I will ever encounter. I commit my writing to You and pray that I will trust You completely to make my paths straight. Amen.*

Reflection

Which of the verses quoted above resonates with you (and your writing)? If you don't have a "theme verse," consider making one of these (or another Proverb) yours.

How do you acknowledge the Lord with your writing?

What can you do to make your words "sweet to the soul and healing to the bones"?

"Let love and faithfulness never leave you; bind them around your neck, write them on the tablet of your heart" (Proverbs 3:3).

God Loves Writers

Writers have always played a key role in God's plan. While ancient Israel was a culture known for its rich oral tradition, they also understood the importance of transcribing these timeless stories into written form. The Hebrew word for scribe is *sopher*. Jewish scribes painstakingly, tirelessly, and accurately copied and recopied Scripture so that it could be handed down to the generations that would live long after them.

"The most important thing I've learned is that persistence and hard work are more important than talent. Talent is a gift, but if it is kept in a box under the bed, it's useless. Many more talented people than I am will never be published because they will never do the work required. I love the idea stage of a novel, that misty place in my imagination where the next book promises to be perfect, the best thing ever written. I love typing *The End* and the relief of knowing I am finally finished. Everything else is hard work." ~Robin Lee Hatcher, best-selling author of *Home in Hart's Crossing* and *The Perfect Life*, www.robinleehatcher.com

Excerpt from "The Trouble with Success"

"Reporters conduct interviews. It is intoxicating. They ask you what it's like to be an author. 'I write much because I am paid little,' you say, and they like that. Your poverty endears you to them. You tell them that the garbage can is a writer's best friend; that writing a book is like driving a car at night. You can't see very far, but you follow the lights. You tell them that writing is the hardest way of earning a living, with the possible exception of loading hand grenades." ~Phil Callaway, humorist, award-winning author of fifteen books, including *Making Life Rich Without Any Money*, www.philcallaway.com

Twenty-seven publishers rejected Dr. Seuss' first book, *And to think I saw it on Mulberry Street,* because it was a little too bizarre. Eventually a publisher took a chance, and the rest is history. In all, Dr. Seuss published forty-eight books and sold more than 250 million copies. Not bad for an author who, when at a loss for a good rhyme, would simply make up a silly new word to fit. ~Source: *The Book of Totally Useless Information* by Don Voorhees

I Give Up

Faith Tibbetts McDonald

"The Lord gave and the Lord has taken away. Blessed be the name of the Lord" (Job 1:21, NAS).

In 1995 our family purchased a four bedroom home so that I could use one bedroom as a writing room. Easy access to a space reserved for writing—a quiet, private get-away from the chattered demands of three young kids—tinted life beautifully for me.

Behind the room's closed door, I sat and gazed out the window. My thoughts roamed, scouting for heart, sense, and motive for expression. Eventually they coalesced and became words on paper.

I *really* wrote in that room. And most of what I wrote was published.

After a few years, conflict escalated between our two boys who shared a bedroom. In order to minimize their interactions, I gave up my writing room so they could each have their own space. I discreetly brushed away tears as we dumped my stuff into a corner of the TV room.

After the move, my writing success diminished. The work I was able to eek out in the noisy TV room, when I wasn't reciting available snack options or mediating skirmishes over the remote, prompted rejection after rejection.

Writing without a space led to frustration and less than my best work. Writing without success led to dejection.

To secure a steady income, my husband urged me to take a teaching opportunity that opened up. It seemed like the right thing to do. Even so, each day as I walked to class, I felt stripped of my calling to write.

Questions rankled my soul. Does God call a writer and then change His mind? Does God assign a writer a mission without providing the means for her to complete it? Had I mistakenly assumed that God had called me to write?

I paged through the Bible to examine stories in which God gave and then required the gift's relinquishment. God asked Abraham to give back Isaac. God allowed Satan to swipe every good gift Job possessed.

It seemed so wrong.

When my anger and grief ebbed, I looked again at God's interactions with Abraham and Job. I saw something new. After requiring, or allowing, relinquishment, God restored and bestowed lavish gifts. Abraham, willing to give one son, gained countless descendants. Of Job, the Bible says, "God made Job prosperous again and gave him twice as much as he had before" (Job 42:10).

In relinquishment, Abraham and Job learned to count on the character of God.

In giving up, I have also learned:

- A Christian writer loves the Caller more than the Calling.
- A successful writer must doggedly pursue her calling in the face of rejection but flexibly serve as God sees fit; whether by writing, teaching, or offering a piece of candy to a student in Jesus' name.

After a time, God often restores. I'm writing this piece in a new writing room my husband built me. It was a few years coming but it's twice as big and twice as nice as the old one. I have *two* windows to gaze out.

But more importantly, I'm writing this piece with a new heart. I want to be like Mary, the mother of Jesus, who, when presented with a gift she hadn't asked for—a gift that would bless all people but would cost her plenty of perplexity and grief—said, "I am the Lord's servant, and I am willing to accept whatever He wants" (Luke 1:38, NLT).

Prayer: *Lord, I am Your servant. Let me write when You say write. Let me pursue other avenues of service when You open the way. Amen.*

Reflection

How do you know you're called to write?

What has God called you to give up for Him?

How can you trust Him today with one thing that you want to hold on to?

"I wish my teachers in college had encouraged me to write and submit for publication while a student. I thought you had to have a bachelor's degree in order to publish anything. Many publications don't require an extensive bio—or even clippings—in order to publish a person. In fact, if we receive a bio with any submission, we toss it." ~Susan King, editor, *The Upper Room*

"In many ways, writing is a test of our faith and endurance. But think what He endured for us. When we develop our endurance, it makes us quite a character and ready for anything. Remember: if He called you to it, He'll bring you through it. Keep on keeping on—let's write! After all, that's what writers do!" ~Charlotte Holt, author of *Praise the Lord for Roaches*

"Are you thinking God used that rejection letter to tell you to quit writing? Honey, He does not work that way. If God wants you doing something else, He'll bless you with the desire to do something else. He will never guide you by hammering you down." ~ Trish Perry, author of *Too Good to Be True* and *The Guy I'm Not Dating*, www.trishperrybooks.com

Dem Bones, Dem Bones, Dem Dry Bones
Debora M. Coty

"This is what the sovereign Lord says to these bones: I will make breath enter you, and you will come to life. I will attach tendons to you and make flesh come upon you and cover you with skin... Then you will know that I am the Lord" (Ezekiel 37:5-7, NIV).

As a little girl growing up in the Deep South, I often sang an old spiritual ballad about God plunking the prophet Ezekiel into a desert valley full of dry bones and then admonishing him to call those old dead bones to life.

"Wha-da-ya-think, 'Zekiel?" God asked (my paraphrase). "Can it be done?"

"Beats me!" I can just picture ole Zeke shaking his head and shrugging tunic-draped shoulders. "Only you know about miracles like that, Lord."

But Ezekiel obeyed God's seemingly ridiculous instructions, and sure enough, amidst a mighty clamor and rattle, the foot bones connected to the...ankle bones, the ankle bones connected to the...leg bones, the leg bones connected to the...hip bones, and before he knew it, God's man was surrounded by a veritable army of clattering skeletons. They formed the framework of real men, but at this point, they were missing something vital.

Much like the pathetic skeleton pirates that Captain Jack Sparrow (Johnny Depp) battled in *Pirates of the Caribbean: Curse of the Black Pearl.* In the light of day they appeared to be heart-beating, blood-pumping humans, but moonlight exposed them for what they really were: a pile of lifeless bones strung together by gristle and shredded pirate garb. The dead masquerading as the living.

Ezekiel realized right away that these spiritless beings before him in the valley of bones were worthless. Without the breath of God to infuse them with life, they were powerless, ineffectual...completely incapable to accomplish any eternal purpose. But God wasn't finished yet.

"Then he said to me, 'Prophesy to the breath; prophesy, son of man, and say to it, 'This is what the Sovereign Lord says: Come from the four winds, O breath, and breathe into these slain, that they might live'" (Ezekiel 37:9).

And live they did.

As writers, we may face the Ezekiel dilemma. We sink countless hours, back-breaking effort, and even frustrated tears into our manuscripts, but sometimes the words just lie there like lifeless bones strung together in a parched paper desert. It's not enough to fabricate the framework, the skeleton, of a mighty work. Without God's breath of life, there the bones will remain—dead words masquerading as living, Holy Spirit-inspired messages. Mere counterfeits of the real thing.

I once wrote an anecdotal short story that I thought was insightful and instructive. I submitted it to a dozen Christian magazines and was turned down flat. An editor at a writer's conference told me the piece was well written, but the take-away just wasn't there. Yet I had learned a valuable spiritual lesson during the real life experience that was described in the story.

I prayed about how to better communicate God's life-lesson and waited. As I was reading my Bible, the simplicity and passion of the scriptural language spoke to me in such a way that I knew what was missing from my story. God's breath of life!

It's now a published article, and readers who have grown through the sharing of my experience remind me that without the Lord's breath of life, dem bones will never escape the desert.

So how do we avoid this literary death trap? This valley of dry bones?

The first and most important step we can take to ensure that our words reflect those of our Heavenly Father is to stay in the Word. Revelation 22:18-19 warns us of dire consequences if we add to or subtract words from Holy Scripture. The only way to respect those parameters is to familiarize ourselves with God's word. Daily Bible reading and reflection not only promote personal spiritual growth but allow us to infuse our writing with the very heartbeat of God: The single, most powerful force that can truly touch souls.

Giving our work to the Lord daily as a love offering helps put our successes and failures into perspective. If God is truly in control, our fretting and worrying and losing sleep is futile. If a needy person is meant to discover God's love through our literary love offerings, it will happen—even through supernatural intervention that defies all logic. If a manuscript is rejected, it's because the Lord, in His infinite foresight, determined that those dry bones weren't ready for His breath of life...yet.

Praying for God's guidance and looking for His answers are essential to the process of fleshing out our skeletons. If God has called us to a writing ministry, He doesn't intend our corpses to rattle forever. Our dry bones must go through a growth process—just like Ezekiel's skeletons when tendons were added to attach muscles that provide power and movement. And then flesh and skin were applied to protect the soft, vulnerable tissue and keep the important core intact.

As we earnestly ask for God's guidance, we may miss His still, small voice if we aren't expecting a reply. Do you know what the missing vital element was for Ezekiel's impotent skeletons? The answer is found in Ezekiel 37:4 and repeated in the last line of the "Dem Bones" song: *"And hear the word of the Lord!"*

Prayer: *Sovereign Breath of Heaven, raise my literary dead bones into a vast living army so that like Ezekiel, I may know You are Lord of all. Amen.*

Reflection

1. What dry bones have you been faced with during the last three months?

2. Have you asked the Lord to breathe his breath into the dry bones in your desert valley? Plan two positive steps you can take toward fleshing out your literary skeletons.

3. Think of a God-breathed literary work that impacted your life (fiction or non-fiction). Locate and re-read it, taking careful notes of the elements that made the

words come alive to you. How can your work be infused with the same life force?

Excerpt from "The Trouble with Success"

"One day you wake up and smell the decaf. It comes in the form of a beautiful letter. 'My life was changed forever...my family and I are following Christ after reading your book.' And you get down on your knees and repent of your whining and give thanks to Almighty God for the privilege and the pains and the joys of being a writer." ~Phil Callaway, humorist, best-selling author of *It's Always Darkest Before the Fridge Door Opens*, www.philcallaway.com

"Always include a large woodshed in your books. It's a good place to stack the bodies should your characters start getting in the way of the story." ~Craig Alan Hart, Founder of "Christian Fiction On-Line"

"The most valuable lesson I've learned about writing is to give my talent to God. Then seek His help with it daily. He created my gift of writing in the first place. He knows better than anyone, including me, how it can best be used." ~Brandilyn Collins, author of *Getting Into Character* and *Coral Moon*, www.brandilynncollins.com

"For those who are willing to make an effort, great miracles and wonderful treasures are in store." ~Isaac Bashevis Singer, Novel Prize-winning writer (1902-1991)

Next Time, Offer Your Lunch
Suzanne Woods Fisher

"Freely you have received, freely give" (Matthew 10:8, NIV).

Jesus' miraculous feeding of the 5,000 with only two fish and five loaves is described in all four gospels. In fact, it's the only miracle, apart from the resurrection, found in all four gospels. John added a few interesting details: a hungry crowd was on its way to listen to Jesus; the only known food was a lunch of small fish and barley loaves. And the lunch belonged to a boy.

Do you think the boy volunteered to offer his lunch? Or was it confiscated by an authoritative disciple looking for a quick visual display to respond to Jesus' ridiculous question? "When Jesus looked up and saw a great crowd coming toward him, he said to Philip, 'Where shall we buy bread for these people to eat'?" (John 6:5)

I can imagine Philip bringing the boy over to Jesus, pulling the napkin off the pail with a flourish to show Jesus the modest meal and exclaim with thinly veiled sarcasm, "Eight months' wages would not buy enough bread for each to have a bite!"

What Philip didn't realize was that Jesus was testing him. "For he already had in mind what he was going to do" (John 6:6). Jesus knew what was in the boy's pail, *and* He knew the boy's heart. Knowing Jesus like we do, it's fair to assume that He would only perform a miracle if the boy had been willing. So...I think the boy freely offered what he had to Jesus.

What if the boy had said no? After all, he was probably from a poor family. That was no lavish lunch; it was merely sustenance. Barley was not as high a quality grain as wheat; it's gritty. And I have a hunch that the two small fish might have been caught by the boy on the way to hear Jesus that morning. Perhaps the boy hoped to roast the fish on a small fire. What if the boy had hidden his pail from those nosy disciples? No one would blame him. After all, he was a growing boy! He needed his nourishment.

But he didn't. He offered to Jesus what he had, and Jesus multiplied it profoundly. "Jesus then took the loaves, gave thanks, and distributed to those who were seated as much as they wanted. He did the same with the fish. When they had all had enough to eat, he said to his disciples, 'Gather the pieces that are left over. Let nothing be wasted.' So they gathered them and filled twelve baskets with the pieces of the five barley loaves left over by those who had eaten." (John 6:12-14).

When they all had enough to eat? That means that over 5,000 people were *satisfied.* Because one boy offered his meager lunch.

Are you a beginner at giving? Especially giving to others from your experience as a writer? Do you feel as if you have nothing to offer anyone else, that you need more seasoning under your belt before you dare to think about mentoring a new writer? Or even to help someone get started?

Or maybe you're worried that if you offer help to someone, say, introducing her to an editor or an agent, it could squeeze out your own chances of publication. After all, it *is* a competitive field. No one would blame you for not offering to help. Right?

Wrong. We don't live by the world's rules. The boy with the fish and loaves didn't. He didn't wait until everything was right to give. He just gave.

As we four writers have been working on *Grit for the Oyster*, we have asked scores of established authors to share their best advice for aspiring writers. Many responded wholeheartedly. They enthusiastically offered advice, encouraged us in our endeavor, and asked to be kept updated on the publication of the book.

Their response has been a remarkable testament to us of the Christian community. We never expected it! And it's taught us to be like those generous authors. *Now.* Not to wait until *Grit for the Oyster* hits the New York Times bestseller list. Or even (as I write this) not to wait until *Grit* is contracted to a publisher. But *now*.

As you have opportunity to help others, give! Be generous. Share your know-how. Edit someone's article. Divulge your tips. Show off your hard-earned battle scars. Even if you don't feel worthy or ready. Just give! And, like the boy who shared his lunch, be prepared for Christ to multiply your generosity in ways you never expected.

Prayer: *Giver of Good Gifts, thank you for the modeling of others to teach us how to give. Today, O Lord, I want to offer to You what I have—cheerfully, diligently, and freely. Amen.*

Reflection

Who has been a generous writer to you? How did he/she help you?

Have you been asked to help another with writing? How did you respond? How did it turn out?

Is there a gift—of time, attention, an encouraging word, a helpful suggestion—that you could offer to another today?

"Every writer I know has had the benefit of those who have come before. EVERY writer. I write the way I do because I was influenced by a handful of successful authors. I had a couple of dedicated teachers who committed themselves to helping me improve my craft. I had writers around me who shared from their experience. All of us are creating things that are derivative—we're all building on the books we've read, the authors we've admired, and the wisdom we've received. So make it a point to share your own story with other writers. Be generous. Help build the next generation of authors." ~Chip MacGregor, agent, MacGregor Literary Agency

"In Scripture, God is the consummate advertiser. Because He knows that nothing can satisfy people like a relationship with himself, He uses the power of word to persuade them to 'buy into' new life with Him. So great is His love for people that He is willing to woo them. For wooing He needs literary language, the kind of language that can touch their hearts." ~Margaret Parker, author of *Unlocking the Power of God's Word*

"Unless a writer works constantly to improve and refine the tools of his trade, they will be useless instruments if and when the moment of inspiration or revelation does come. This is the moment when a writer is spoken through, the moment that a writer must accept with gratitude and humility, and then attempt, as best he can, to communicate to others." ~Madeleine L'Engle, best-selling author, excerpted from her Newbery Medal acceptance speech, www.madeleinelengle.com

"Thank God that throughout history He hasn't always used the ones who please Him, He uses whoever He pleases. Even you." ~Phil Callaway, humorist, author of *Laughing Matters* and *Family Squeeze,* www.philcallaway.com

On Our Bookshelves: *Favorite Must-Haves*

Christian Writer's Market Guide by Sally Stuart (Waterbrook).Get the most recent version each and every year. (Suzanne's pick)

Self-Editing for Fiction Writers by Renni Browne and Dave King (Harper Resource). A highly recommended guide from many writing conferences; immeasurably helpful. (Debora's pick)

Words Fail Me by Patricia O'Connor (Harvest/HBJ Book). This is a witty and helpful book that inspires readers to try hard to be better writers. (Joanna's pick)

Bird by Bird: Some Instructions on Writing and Life by Anne Lamott (Anchor). True to Lamott's quirky and autobiographical style, this book is filled with insights and wisdom about the writing life.(Suzanne's pick)

The Elements of Style by William Strunk Jr. and E.B.White (Longman). A classic must-have for writers of every genre.(Debora's pick)

The Writer Within: A Guide to Creative Non-fiction by Lary Bloom (Bibliopola Press).This book will help you believe in your dream to write and encourage you to pursue your passion. (Faith's pick)

Woe is I: The Grammarphobe's Guide to Better English in Plain English by Patricia T. O'Conner (Riverhead Books). Readable, enjoyable, accurate. (Suzanne's pick)

How to Be Your Own Literary Agent by Richard Curtis (Houghton Mifflin Company). Writer's Digest calls it "required reading" and I agree; written from an insider's perspective, it's an excellent tool to understand the nitty gritty of the publishing industry. (Debora's pick)

If You Want to Write: A Book about Art, Independence and Spirit by Brenda Ueland (Graywolf Press). An inspiring book to jumpstart your confidence. (Suzanne's pick)

On Writing Well by William Zinsser (Quill A HarperResource Book). Sound advice on writing to the best of your ability. A classic. (Faith's pick)

The Dictionary of Concise Writing:10,000 Alternatives to Wordy Phrases, by Robert Hartwell Fiske (Marion Street Press, Inc.). An indispensable guide to writing well. (Joanna's pick)

Book Proposals That Sell by W. Terry Whalin (Write Now Publications). A helpful book for non-fiction writers filled with insider know-how about the publishing world. (Debora's pick)

Getting the Words Right by Theodore A. Rees Cheney (Writer's Digest Books). A book about writing concisely. (Faith's pick)

How to Write a Book Proposal by Michael Larsen, AAR (1997), Cincinnati: Writer's Digest Books. (Joanna's pick)

Bible Quotation References

The Holy Bible quotations are from the following translations:

1. *The Living Bible* (TLB), copyright ©1971 by Tyndale House Publishers, Wheaton, Ill. Used by permission.

2. *The Holy Bible, New International Version* ® (NIV), copyright ©1973, 1978, 1984 by International Bible Society. Used by permission of Zondervan Bible Publishing House. All rights reserved.

3. *Contemporary English Version* (CEV), copyright © 1995, American Bible Society. Used by permission.

4. *The Message* (TM), copyright © 1993,1994,1995,1996,2000,2001,2002. Used by permission of NavPress Publishing Group. Published by NavPress, Colorado Springs, CO 80935.

5. *New American Standard Bible* (NASB), copyright ©1960, 1962, 1963, 1968, 1971, 1972, 1973, 1975, 1977 by the Lockman Foundation. Used by permission.

6. *Holy Bible, New Living Translation* (NLT), copyright © 1996. Used by permission of Tyndale House Publishers, Inc., Wheaton, ILL 80189. All rights reserved.

7. *New King James Version* (NKJV), copyright © 1979, 1980, 1982 by Thomas Nelson, Inc. Used by Permission. All rights reserved.

Coming January 30, 2008 from Vintage Spirit

I See God in the Simple Things
A Devotional Journal
Shirley Kiger Connolly

In all we experience through simple daily living, God faithfully shows us more about ourselves and where we are in our spiritual walks. Too often we allow complicated days to dominate our lives, making it difficult to cope. What lesson is God teaching you about your life today?

This lighthearted book of reflections illustrates through words how every day situations can turn into opportunities for encouragement and spiritual growth. Each lesson provides us with a moment to go to God for answers, to gain insight from His Word, and to share our own personal thoughts no matter how mundane or troublesome they appear.